The Native Daughter

Stories drawn from real life: history through a child's eyes, showing the quiet strength individuals and families carry.

———

Within these pages, you will find:

- An understanding of how identity is formed before we have language for it
- The quiet endurance of women and children moving through history silently
- The ways movement, loss, and care can coexist
- Roots are not carried as places, but as lived experiences
- The early arrival of love and responsibility in a child's life
- Men striving to preserve family under forces beyond their control

Also By Wanjirũ Warama

BOOKS

Unexpected America

Entangled in America

Years of Shame (a 3-story novella)

Beyond Conscious Self (a two-story Novelette)

The Colonial Farm

The Native Daughter

SHORT STORIES

New Beginning: Why Religion Never Appealed to Me Until…

ANTHOLOGY

Why Religion Never Appealed to Me Until… (Personal Essay – San Diego Writers and Editors Guild 2023 Anthology)

The Native Daughter

A Memoir of Movement and Change

Wanjirũ Warama

Athomi Books
San Diego, California, USA

The Native Daughter

Copyright © 2026 by Wanjirũ Warama
All rights reserved.

No part of this book may be reproduced, transmitted, or utilized in any form or by any means, electronic or mechanical, now known or hereafter invented, including photocopying, recording, or any information storage or retrieval system, without prior written permission of the copyright holder.

Published by Athomi Books
8064 Allison Ave, #684
La Mesa, CA 91942
United States of America

February 17, 2026

First Edition
Library of Congress Control Number: 2026900540

ISBN: 978-1-954423-15-2 (Paperback)
ISBN: 978-1-954423-17-6 (Hardcover)
ISBN: 978-1-954423-16-9 (eBook)

Cover design by eBookLaunch.com

wanjiruwarama.com

...

Dedication

To my late parents, Warama wa Njerũ and Mary Nyachuru Ndurumo Warama, who did their best under extraordinary political and economic conditions.

A river that forgets its source will dry up.
—African Proverb.

Contents

Author's note

The Native Daughter is a work of nonfiction; these stories are true. They unfolded not just in my life, but in the lives of my siblings, my parents, and our entire community. While I have striven for factual accuracy, drawing on historical records where possible, this is ultimately a story of shared memory—filtered through time and individual perspective.

My goal here is to honor the spirit and the emotional truth of those moments, inviting you to experience the world as we lived it.

—Wanjirũ Warama

...

Early Memories

1. Bus to Nakuru -1956

Wawerũ snuggled on my back in a ngoi, its strap across my tender head. In Mother's absence, Ndurumo, my fifteen-year-old brother, took her place. He threw a piece of cloth over the baby and helped me tie it around my chest to reinforce the baby carrier. I then joined my father, who was waiting in the courtyard.

He and I left the village early that morning to catch the only bus between Solai and Nakuru Town. The dew on the footpath through the savanna wet my feet, but only for a short distance before we branched onto a dirt and stunted-grass tractor trail, an occasional fixture on colonial farms in Kenya.

On the two miles to the bus stop, my heart warmed in anticipation of my first bus ride. I had never ridden in a motor vehicle before. At the roadside, I kept an eye down the road, eager to enjoy the ride for all eighteen miles to town.

Will the trip last the entire day? I asked myself. That would be such a thrill.

Before long, intermittent honks, like those of a harmonica, alerted us; the bottom-blue and top-white bus appeared. The driver could have saved his honks. With no other cars on the dirt country road, no one could have missed the dust that fouled the fresh, cool air we had enjoyed since we left home.

When we boarded, the conductor directed us to vacant seats in the middle. My father (my Baba) stood in the aisle so I could sit first. The bus started moving. "Hurry," he said as he held onto two seat frames. I scooted under his arm, sat on the edge of the seat, and swiveled Wawerũ to my front the way Mother and other village women did when they prepared to sit or carry loads on their backs. I then leaned back, and my little brother's temple rested on my chest.

Baba took the seat behind mine, his hat on, still clad in his employer's issued winter-like gray coat.

Two makanga (baggage handlers) sat in front. Whenever our bus stopped, they rushed off to unload or load the passengers' luggage in the overhead carrier and the compartment at the rear of the bus.

A third man, who had shown us to our seats, sat alone across from the makanga. He collected bus fare and gave change.

Anyone who spoke on that bus spoke in Gĩkũyũ.

Since we left home, Wawerũ slept or looked at me with sunken eyes, his body lethargic—too sick to cry or want food. I had wished Mother were home; she would have given him medicine, and he wouldn't be that ill. But on the bus, I stopped worrying. I knew hospital people would treat him.

I now occupied myself by looking at trees zooming by backward as our bus sped on. The sight fascinated me, and soon the motion soothed me, making me doze on and off.

We came to a fork, where a tarmac road split into two dirt roads—the one our bus drove on and another, almost parallel to ours, that looped northwards.

The conductor called out, "Mailikumi! Mailikumi!" (Ten Miles! Ten Miles!) Baba leaned toward me and pointed. "That road goes to Bahati Market," he said, "and all the way to Nyeri. This stage is ten miles from Nakuru Town. That's where the tarmac road goes."

I craned my neck and looked, without saying anything. He didn't expect me to.

The driver parked the bus on a well-beaten shoulder. We remained there for about five minutes while people got off and others boarded.

When the bus entered the wider tarmac road, the ride became smoother. I released my grip on the side of my seat and sat upright. I relished a countryside dotted with dust-free trees and greenery, and an occasional herd of black-and-white cows or goats scattered across the rambling landscape of the various European colonial farms. I felt a thrill when vehicles zoomed by, but I wished our bus driver would drive faster.

Before we arrived in town, the bus entered a tarmacked and wider road where cars and lorries drove in one direction only. Passengers said it was the Nakuru/Nairobi Road. Another road ran parallel to ours, farther on, where cars headed in the opposite direction.

Trees that I learned years later were jacarandas lined the strip of land between the two roads. Purple flowers sprouted on their crowns as if they were giant bouquets. The trees looked as if somebody had planted them, along with the well-trimmed grass that carpeted the ground.

I doubted anyone planted trees in Solai. But all kinds of indigenous trees, like mũrema, mũkũyũ, and mũtamaiyũ, in different sizes and shapes, along with various grasses, shrubs, creepers, and even wild fruits like blackberries and gooseberries, grew or intertwined just as nature created them. Did I prefer the jacarandas and managed landscape over the free-for-all Solai vegetation? Not really. On my first time out of the farm, it never occurred to me to compare or consider that.

As our bus entered Nakuru, blooming bougainvillea lined the street. We ended up at a roundabout. I hung onto the seat's frame so I would not slide into the aisle. The town came into full view. It looked clean, as if townspeople swept and washed it daily—unlike our dirt road and footpaths. I saw more cars and buses than I thought existed. Pedestrians hurried back and forth. As we neared the bus terminal, some walked confidently so close to vehicles that drivers could have run them over. But they didn't.

The terminal filled with parked buses, and makanga shouted their destinations. Ours shouted, "Mwisho! Mwisho!" (Last stop! Last stop!) When the bus slowed toward its designated parking spot, the luggage handlers opened the door and hopped out before the driver parked. To get off the bus, I held onto the seat frame and swiveled Wawerũ onto my back.

From the bus station, Baba held my hand—the only time he did so, unless I count the first time, which I'll ignore for now, the afternoon he whipped me with a twig when I was four. All I can say and wallow in is that I felt safe and anchored when he held my hand this second and final time. He helped me cross two streets as we weaved back the way our bus had come. He dropped it when we reached the curb by the roundabout.

I stayed close behind him as we walked on the shoulder of the Nairobi/Nakuru road. We covered about a quarter of a mile before turning onto another jacaranda-lined street that led us to Nakuru General Hospital.

Even hospital people grew trees, hedges, flowers, and well-trimmed grass between the rectangular stone buildings with red or green-tiled rooftops. Baba marched toward the waiting room as if he were going home.

I am unsure how long we waited, seated on benches along the corridor with others—mainly barefoot rural women hugging their sick children—before a nurse came to get us. She led us to a room where we found a white doctor. She offered the two chairs by the doctor's desk and stood aside between the doctor and us.

He asked questions in his language, a language I had never heard before, which I soon learned was English. The doctor's look fascinated me more than his language. I kept stealing glances at him, maybe even gawked, wishing I could touch and feel his fragile-looking, skinless hand. Would he feel pain? I wondered. It was my second time seeing a white person. My first sighting was at my mother's job three years prior. Awe and fear had struck me, but that was from at least thirty feet away.

Years later, when I finally touched a white person's hand, I learned how mistaken I had been. It turned out to be skin like any other.

Now, the nurse translated the doctor's words into Gĩkũyũ for Baba. Besides saying, "Ndĩroimire wĩra ira ndĩrakora mwana emũrũaru" (I returned from work yesterday and found the child sick), Baba did not seem to know what else to say. The doctor rounded his desk and stooped over where I held Wawerũ in my lap. He opened and looked at each of Wawerũ's withered eyes before he put a stethoscope to his chest and listened.

"What happened to your brother?" the nurse asked me.

"He's sick and doesn't want to eat," I said, "and he watches me with half-open eyes."

After the check-up, the doctor spoke with the nurse. The nurse turned to Baba. "The doctor says your son is too sick to return home," she said. "But he's too young to stay in the hospital alone."

I listened, confused.

"What does he want me to do?" Baba asked.

"He has admitted both of your children."

How could that be? I'm not sick. I turned and looked up at my father to assess his reaction. He turned toward me. "The hospital will look after you and your brother," he said.

"Okay," I said. If Baba said it was okay, it was all right.

The doctor finished writing his instructions and gave the papers to the nurse. To my relief, she took Wawerū from me and directed his head to rest on her shoulder. "Ndūkamake. Nī tūkorora chiana chiaku wega," (Don't worry; we'll take care of your children well), she told Baba.

"Nīwega mūno" (Thank you very much), Baba replied, then faced me. "Look out for your brother. I'll return to check on you," he said before he turned and left.

"Let's go," the nurse told me.

I quickened my steps to keep up with her along the corridor while my mind churned. For a tiny nine-year-old girl, I had experienced more than my fair share of life. And of all my parents' dreams for me, their first daughter, I doubt either of them expected me at my age to pad on hospital hallways on a mission to act as a surrogate mother to my little brother.

But there I was.

2. The Homestead

Nine years before the hospital trip—long before we moved to the village where we now lived—I had taken my first breath on a farm owned by Kamunge, one of the original British colonizers. My parents named me Wanjirũ after my paternal grandmother. Had I been born in Nyeri, their ancestral homeland, when the Gĩkũyũ Nation was still intact, as a native daughter, the two midwives who attended to my mother would have announced my arrival with four ululations; boys received five.

But things had changed. Still, by that fluke of birth order, I became the first daughter, which gave me an edge above any future daughters but below the sons and, of course, eons below the British.

My family lived at Kĩrĩma-inĩ (by the mountain), a homestead nestled in the far western corner of the colonial farm, with no neighbors for at least two miles. A quarter mile to the west, the land sloped sharply to the Tindaress River, where Baba's goats drank and where we drew our water.

Women in my family filled their five-gallon cylindrical tin containers, tied them with leather straps at opposite ends, and hoisted them onto their backs with straps across their heads. They then inched back up the incline—like climbing a mountain—hence the name Kĩrĩma-inĩ. If a woman failed to arch her back enough and hang onto the strap by her ears, her container could roll off, endanger her legs, and tumble down the river.

Lucky for me, political turmoil broke out in Kenya, and the farm owner ordered us to move before I grew old enough to tackle that incline.

*

Our compound, a traditional circular homestead of the Gĩkũyũ people with a central courtyard, comprised five houses. Baba lived in a thingira (man's house—boys' and goats' cottages were also thingiras but prefixed accordingly). His thingira was strategically built to offer a view of the entire courtyard.

Nyũmba, the largest house, belonged to my mother (as a girl's house would). She and her children used it as the living room, kitchen, and bedroom. At night, Mother shared it with her youngest children until they moved to the boys' thingira. But when her two girls—Nyandia and I—came along, nyũmba became our permanent sleeping quarters.

My three brothers shared an unpartitioned thingira, and the goats shared their own. Some of Baba's goats occupied the fifth house that Kaguyu, Baba's ex-wife, had lived in before. Our stick-and-mud-plastered circular houses had conical thatched roofs. Because of its larger size, nyũmba had the thickest central supporting wood pillar extending about a foot above the peak.

The houses contained no windows, except for the three- or four-inch gaps between the rafters and the walls. These provided ventilation, as did the doors, which remained ajar until dusk. Ventilation failed only when someone used wet firewood or wood that was not bone-dry; then the smoke became excessive and stung our eyes. We blew at it or fanned it away from our faces. A cough or sneeze never trailed far from us, especially when Mother tended the fire. Despite all that smoke, I don't recall catching a single cold when we lived there.

Writers often call such houses huts. To us, they were suitable and comfortable dwellings—warm during the cold months and cool during the hot ones. Besides, families like mine lived at the employer's pleasure. He could order a move at a moment's notice. My parents knew this was always possible, but they never expected it. They were taken by surprise when the order came for us to move.

The granary, the only structure free of mud, had walls woven from dry vines and a grass-thatched roof. Raised on stilts to allow ventilation and deter animals, it stored maize, beans, peas, potatoes, seeds for the next year, empty bags, tools, and various items. With no refrigeration and nyũmba too warm, Mother also stored cooked food there for the family to eat over several days. Next came the chicken coop, smaller and built of wood and chicken wire.

All structures faced the courtyard, fenced with dry wooden sticks reinforced by shrubs and creepers. These filled holes caused by age or by Baba's he-goats when they waged their wars, head-butting each other for a doe. The winner took the doe. The female had no say in the matter.

The gate, with two posts on each side and ladder-like rungs, completed the compound. It stayed open from morning to evening. Before dusk, after the chickens and goats turned in, Baba or my older brothers slid several long poles across the entrance, the bottom ones close enough to keep out anything larger than a chicken or a cat.

My parents went to work early every morning for Kamunge, six days a week. Sunday was their day of rest, when they tended to chores or ran their businesses. Mother sold snuff tobacco, and Baba sold hides and skin straps used by women to carry firewood or water.

On two Sundays each month, they woke up at the first cock-crow and walked seven miles to Kabazi Market on the other side of Jumatatu Mountain. After payday, they walked ten miles to the bigger Bahati Market.

When my parents returned home, Mother cooked and took care of household chores. But Baba needed a break after the long trek under the equatorial sun. He rested, drank njohi, his homemade beer, and admired his herd of animals when they returned from pasture.

3. My Earliest Memory

My life is dotted with distinct islands of memories and blurs. One of my earliest foggy moments was when I saw a strange woman standing on thingira's porch. Confused, I gawked at her. I failed to understand her status or significance in our family. I remained confused even after I learned who she was. Understanding her place in our family would take many more years.

Decades later, when reminiscing with my brother Ndurumo about our family, he told me about another incident. "You were a stubborn child," he said.

"Why do you say that?" I asked.

"If I let you, you'd have latched onto my back until you were four or older."

It so happened that Ndurumo babysat me and also herded our father's goats. He carried me wherever he took the herd across the sprawling savanna.

During one incident, about the period I saw the woman by Baba's thingira, Ndurumo and I reached a clear footpath where he put me down. "You can walk now," he said.

I balked and pursed my lips.

"Let's go," he said and took a few steps forward.

Instead of following him, I slumped cross-legged in the middle of the trail and tightened my lips, ready to summon tears.

He walked on, rounded the bend, and disappeared behind wiregrass and scanty shrubs.

It's hard to tell what I was thinking, but it's safe to say I was determined not to move a single step.

About a minute later, I caught Ndurumo stooped, peering from the tall wiregrass. When I noticed him, he backed away. After two times, he realized the trick wouldn't work on me. He marched toward me, arguing with himself, "about this stubborn child." He grabbed me by the arm and angrily threw me on his back, hitched me up to ensure I stayed there, and boisterously marched on. I quickly latched onto his shoulders.

These memories, scattered and half-formed, were the first traces of the child I once was: determined, bewildered, and still discovering my place in the world.

A clearer memory, however, the one that marked the beginning of my understanding, came from a completely different kind of trouble.

4. The Fear of Woods

My first concrete troublesome memory came about because we used the sprawling wooded area outside our compound as our toilet. I can only speculate why my parents did not think to dig a toilet. Or they did not know we needed one amid all that wooded country.

To potty-train me, Mother led me outside the gate, walked along a footpath about ten to twenty yards from the homestead, pointed me to a spot inland, and stood to watch like a sentry. Training ceased when I turned four years old after the birth of my little brother, Gĩthũi. Mother had trained me well by then, but the vast wild thicket of trees, shrubs, and tall grass out-side—spreading for miles, it seemed—intimidated me. Left without support, I improvised.

Whenever the urge hit me, I looked this way and that before I sneaked to the farthest part of the fence close to nyũmba and deposited my little turds.

The first time Mother discovered a mound before the chick-ens cleared my deposit, she scooped it with velvety maigoya leaves from the fencing shrubs.

"You're old enough to know better," she said, wagging her index finger at me. She promised dire consequences if it happened again.

I did not mean to defy my mother; I merely wanted to get relief without fear. But now that she had found out my secret, I needed to devise secure hideouts where I could sneak in undetected.

My sister Nyandia was two years old, too young to snitch on me. Machira, two years older than me, preferred to join goat herders in the savanna or to romp outdoors farther than the courtyard.

Feeling safe, a dash under the eaves behind nyũmba became my new strategy. To my dismay, the minute Mother reached her doorway, coming from the granary, she stopped, scrunched her face, and sniffed this way and that. She set down gĩtarũrũ (woven tray) and walked four steps toward one side of her house, stopped, sniffed, and said nothing. Then turned and walked a few steps toward the other side, sniffed, sniffed. "Has this child become dumber as she gets older?" my mother shrieked. "She has turned this homestead into a toilet."

"How can she tell?" I asked myself.

"Wanjirũ! Come here!"

She stood by my pile, which now revolted me.

"Get maigoya and clean up your mess!"

I trotted to the fence and plucked leaves, the best I could, one by one, and started whimpering.

"That's enough," she said.

I hurried back, my little hands loaded, my face contorted, and my lips puckered. I stood opposite Mother, my head hung.

"Go on. Scoop it."

Unmotivated, I looked up at her face to ensure she meant it. "Go on," she said.

I bent over, my sniffles louder. My shaky, poorly coordinated hands trembled.

Mother yanked the leaves from me just in the nick of time.

"If you poop anywhere around or inside this courtyard again," she warned as she plucked more leaves, "you'll scoop it with your bare hands."

I looked up at my mother, wide-eyed, and increased the volume of my whimpers. With bare hands? She can't be serious, I thought.

Her warning worried me, but the vast expanse woody area outside our compound worried me more. Even at four, going on five, I kept quiet rather than tell my mother about the fear that shook my little heart, knowing she would minimize or brush aside my concerns, claiming I was old enough.

So, my mother's reprimands and warnings failed to take hold. Whether I braved the grassy area in between is lost to memory. But I recall that whenever I felt the urge, I dashed to wherever I thought my secret was safest.

Soon, I ran out of ways to outwit my mother.

When the next opportunity rolled around, like a revelation, I realized nyũmba—my mother's maze-like house to my young eyes—would solve my dilemma.

It covered approximately 700 square feet, partitioned into three rooms, two of which were semi-dark unless someone used a lantern.

On entering, one came to kweerũ, or foyer, which faced a wall with two entrances. Each entrance led to the living area, which held the fire pit near the center pillar. We often used the larger right entrance because it let in more light. It was also the entrance to the small hallway that separated our mother's bedroom from the tiny room where my sister Nyandia and I shared a bed.

I entered through the larger entrance and skulked like a little stalker to ensure no one remained indoors. I then headed toward the sleeping area, which was difficult for anyone unfamiliar with Mother's bedroom to navigate. But she and I had shared her bed until I turned two years old. I could feel my way around, even if I shut my eyes.

I left my package in the darkest corner, sure Mother would never find out. I believed she possessed special powers that enabled her to discover things, but I doubted she could be that good. I returned to the courtyard and soon forgot my secret.

To my horror, when Mother entered her bedroom, her reaction reached the porch where my sister and I sat doing child stuff.

"This child has done it again! Wanjirū!" Mother called out as she rushed back to the doorway. I stood when she appeared, my now idle hands close to my mouth, aware she had found my hideaway.

"What did I tell you?"

I had forgotten what she had told me. I stared at her, my lower lip curled, my scrunched face full of misery.

"I said you would scoop it with your bare hands."

Oh, yes, I then remembered. I strung out a series of whimpers.

"Is this child getting dumber?" my mother asked, shaking her head, loud enough for anyone in the courtyard to hear.

Her boisterous complaints alerted Baba, who liked to join fights even when they didn't concern him.

He stopped puttering near his thingira and marched toward me, grabbed my right arm, and dragged me along while I trotted behind to keep up.

At the shrubbery by the fence, he broke off a couple of stout twigs and started whipping my buttocks. I dropped to the ground, crossed my legs, and rocked side to side as I screamed and screamed. My eyes followed the path of the lashes, which landed on my exposed thighs while the hem of my little dress flew in all directions, my arms caught in the fracas. He spared my head, perhaps because of my tender age.

I learned much later that Mother had said her children's heads were no-beat zones because she did not want them to grow up demented. But from an assault I witnessed five years later and others I learned about, she had little say about the beatings her children endured at the hands of her husband.

However, Mother tried to intervene on my behalf that one time.

"Run! Run! Run!" she said from yards away.

I saw her hand gestures and heard her voice, but nothing registered.

"This is a stubborn child," Baba said. He shook his head as he tossed his weapon by the fence and walked away.

Soon, my screams ran out of fuel, and I settled for whimpers. I rose and shuffled to the farthest side from the gate and leaned my bruised body against the fence, my breath shuddering.

What does stubborn mean? I wondered. How do I stop it?

While I willed my muscles' throbs to stop, I resolved to brave the woods. Better to outrun the big ogre that ate naughty children that Mother had threatened us with than suffer such pain.

Despite the pain, another question pulsed in my young mind: Why didn't Mother rush in and stop Baba from hurting me?

Much later, as an adult, I would understand the truth about the answer to my question, the truth about patriarchy, even among the colonized.

I often think about that now when I see a child hesitate, withdraw, or act in ways adults dismiss as "naughty." There is always a reason—fear, confusion, or a worry too small to name yet too large to bear alone.

If anyone had asked me what troubled me, or held my hand the way Baba did in town, the path outside our compound might not have seemed so terrifying.

5. Hierarchy of Freedoms

After my early lesson about fear and consequences, I became more aware of the rhythms of our homestead and of who, in our small world, enjoyed freedom and who did not.

My siblings and I enjoyed playing in the courtyard, especially before dusk or during moonlight. On some Saturday or Sunday evenings, Baba sat on a three-legged stool on his porch, his hat on his folded knee, from where he watched. At such times, we refrained or toned down our play.

Sometimes, when I forgot myself and played with unbridled energy, I stopped when I noticed his presence. I then threw him a glance to check whether he had seen me.

We harbored a visceral fear of Baba, passed down from his older children. They viewed him as a disgruntled Superman or a stern god. Nobody dared cross a god. Before the age of seven, however, I had not yet developed that fear; I just followed my brothers' cues.

Yet even as a child, I sensed that when goats romped and we played alongside them, Baba never complained or reprimanded us. Tranquility reigned in the courtyard, and he seemed peaceful as he watched his goats and children play.

Goats, unlike us, enjoyed special treatment without reprimand or concern about who watched them. Well, except for three poor souls imprisoned in a four-foot-high wooden enclosure in nyũmba. Their ballooning bodies could not lie down without stepping or bumping into each other. They lived in that enclosure day and night without a single chance to step outdoors to bask in the sun or stretch their legs. If one did, it was on the way to the slaughter.

Besides an accidental glimpse of those goats through the tiny cracks, I noticed the captives only from their grunts, munches, or bumps.

My mother fed them a variety of green cuttings, potato peels, vegetable remnants, and water. Their stench permeated every clump of dirt and everything else in nyũmba and even wafted into the courtyard to mix with the other goats' and chickens' smells. It did not bother us. We got used to those smells, like dog and other animal owners.

When I grew old enough to question things around me, I failed to understand why those goats never joined the herd in the pasture. Later in my pre-teen years, I learned colonial laws forbade Africans from raising billy or nanny goats.

Agĩkũyũ, however, had always segregated and fattened goats for slaughter on special occasions—engagement parties, the birth of a child, sacrifices, and others. I never witnessed such an event because life on the colonial farm was not conducive to ceremonies or, if one organized one, the farm owner could accuse them of practicing paganism or witchcraft. Although Baba tried to hang onto some traditional remnants before we moved to the village. According to Mother, when I was a toddler, he took my two older brothers—Njerŭ, ten, and Ndurumo, eight—for a male-bonding camping trip, just the three of them, in the woods for three days. They lived on meat and herbal soups from a goat they took with them.

Otherwise, ordinary goats that slept in their cottage enjoyed total freedom. In the mornings before they left for pasture, and especially in the evenings before their bedtime, they stretched, socialized, suckled their young, stole, and ate anything edible we left lying around the courtyard. They fought, bleated, or made love without concern for Baba's reprimand. Well, unless it was a weekend when he craved meat—especially when he drank— and then cut the throat of an unlucky goat.

Chickens seemed the freest members of our household. Perhaps our two cats—one gray and one spotted—could have disagreed. Unbeknownst to them, however, they were working animals. Long before my brothers grew old enough to hone their hunting skills, our two cats were already avid hunters. They let no rodents venture into or close to our courtyard. Any brave that did turned into that day's meal.

Freedom, therefore, belonged to the chickens: no herding off to pasture, no reprimands or beatings, and no chores. They came and went as they pleased, rested under houses or fence shade in the courtyard, or roamed in the surrounding grassland pecking on wild fruit and berries and defenseless insects and larvae until evening. They also ate stray grains or the maize that Mother fed them.

While hens provided eggs, the roosters kept time. Mother often relied on their timekeeping service, especially on market days when she needed to wake earlier than usual. The roosters' crows became a point of reference—whether something happened before or after the first, second, or third crow.

Besides, chickens never went astray like goats or waited for anyone to fetch them. At dusk, they hurried home to beat the darkness as if a predator were chasing them. As a child, it fascinated me to watch a mother hen spew a series of cackles as she hurried back and forth, gathering her chicks.

The minute the chickens piled into their coop, the able-bodied perched on a two-foot-high stick bed across the coop. They disliked sleeping on the floor. But the weak and mother hens had little choice. They headed to safe corners to avoid poop from overhead. A commotion ensued while the overhead chickens slipped before they settled themselves, and the chicks scrambled under their mothers' wings.

Soon, the whole chicken community fell quiet and snoozed. But a chicken could wake up at a moment's notice when it lost its footing or slept with one eye open.

As I understand it now, chickens do not suffer from insomnia worries. Unlike humans, insufficient sleep does not cause side effects in them because they can rest one half of their brain at a time. But keep in mind this is from scientists, humans, not from the chickens.

Besides the freedom our chickens enjoyed, few worried about an untimely death. For undisclosed reasons, Baba never ate wildlife, which, according to him, included chickens. As the head of our household, he owned the chickens, and no one could eat them—at least not openly—without his permission. So, the chickens made merry, bred, and multiplied.

"Warama has a lot of chickens," the family and an occasional visitor said.

While my family looked at the abundance with greedy eyes, Baba watched and admired mahiũ make (his animal wealth). He never remembered—or it never occurred to him—to tell Mother to slaughter a chicken. She had to nudge him to remind him that his children missed the delicacy. Even then, he sometimes took days to respond, perhaps to prove he did not bow to a woman's wish.

But my three older brothers—Njerũ, thirteen; Ndurumo, eleven; and Machira, seven—did not wait for the mind-power games between my parents to play out. When they found a chance to eat chicken, they ate a chicken. They picked a Saturday when Njerũ was out of school, and my parents were at work. Somehow, my sister Nyandia and I failed to notice. Perhaps my brothers just navigated around us.

Machira remained in the woods, minding the goats, while Njerũ and Ndurumo returned home to carry out their heist.

They kindled a fire in nyũmba and left a large pot of water on. Outside, they hunted for a hen without chicks—a breeder lived to old age. They avoided roosters; they were always fewer than the hens, and our parents might have noticed their absence. When they located a suitable victim, they cornered and grabbed the poor hen. One brother strangled it with his bare hands, a practice against our family's meat culture.

Baba would enlighten us once we moved to the village, and I was old enough to pay attention. A legitimate butcher, he told us, cuts the throat and holds the animal steady until the last drop of blood drains from the body. My brothers already knew this, but they could not gamble on accidental sputters.

The strangler dunked the chicken headfirst, with the legs sticking out for easy turning and handling. When they estimated one side of the chicken was cooked, they rolled it over.

Nervous, one of them occasionally went outside to check whether the smell had reached the courtyard or peeked around in case someone or one of my parents returned home.

When they determined the chicken was cooked, Njerū pulled it out by the legs, waited for the water to drain without burning himself, and carried the feast to the woods. He and Machira plucked the chicken over a bed of leafy branch cuttings.

Meanwhile, Ndurumo poured the hot water outside the gate, where a rogue feather would not raise suspicion. He then washed the pot and put it back with the others. Finally, he scanned the inside of the house for any stray evidence, ensuring it was exactly as they had found it.

Not once did my parents notice a single chicken missing.

It wasn't until my brothers reached their late teens—safely past their rites of passage and the era of Baba's beatings—that they finally shared the story with Mother and us children. We showered them with pure admiration for their ingenuity.

"I should have devised a way to feed my children all those chickens," Mother quipped.

Nobody dared or cared to enlighten Baba, who remained in the dark then and forever.

6. Njerũ

Among us children, freedom had its own hierarchy; no one embodied that uneven balance more than my oldest brother, Njerũ—the boy who seemed destined for both trouble and survival in equal measure.

Too young to appreciate my three brothers' exploits, I watched them with envy as they pranked each other and sprinted around the courtyard. I longed to join them. But Machira, two years older, dismissed me with the ease of a boy who preferred the company of other boys; little sisters were an inconvenience.

I knew Ndurumo and Machira herded goats, and that Njerũ spent most of his days elsewhere. Only later, when we moved to the village, did I understand he had spent his weekdays at a place called school and on weekends had joined the other two to take the goats to pasture.

From the boisterous freedom my three dear brothers enjoyed, one would think they harbored no worries. But as they grew older, besides Baba's violence toward them, which I had not yet witnessed, more unpleasant incidents drifted into their lives.

Njerũ, especially, seemed to have a monopoly on early traumas. His first spell came after Ndurumo's birth. Within a week, he quit eating, stopped thriving, and regressed to a silent baby — listless, unable to talk, cry, or walk.

Mother massaged his shrinking body with warm castor oil while Baba scavenged for medicinal herbs. She boiled the herbs and fed him sips of the liquid. When their efforts failed, they consulted one medicine man, then another. Perhaps it was a curse from the ancestors. Baba slaughtered a goat to appease them, but nothing worked. Njerũ continued to wither.

Mother gave up hope but force-fed him teaspoons of goat's milk or porridge while she waited for him to die.

"I wanted to try anything I could to save my child," she said later.

After three months, Njerũ surprised her. Like a wilted plant revived by sudden rain, he emerged from the stupor and slowly began to eat. Within a month, he resumed his place in the world as a bouncy, handsome toddler.

The family called it a mystery.

Decades later, when I asked Njerũ about that illness, he told me with vigor the same story about the "mystery." I resisted sharing my suspicion that he might have suffered from severe abandonment when Mother's singular focus on him shifted to the newborn baby.

*

Like my three brothers, as a baby, I accompanied Mother to her job or to the garden. Meanwhile, the family relegated Njerũ's mysterious illness to the background. Mother usually left Ndurumo, Machira, and him at home and asked one of our half-siblings from Baba's first family, who lived behind our compound, to keep an eye on them.

One late afternoon, Njerũ and Ndurumo played hide-and-seek around the courtyard while Machira tagged along. They ducked behind or under anything that could conceal them. After several rounds, they ran out of hiding places. When Njerũ's turn came again, he figured one place Ndurumo would never suspect.

"Shut your eyes," he told Ndurumo.

Njeru then rounded to the front, stepped on the granary's jutting boards, opened the small, creaky door, and slipped inside. He rummaged through Mother's bags and the household tools. Before long, a "beehive" distracted him.

Bees had colonized an empty four-gallon gourd in which Mother stored grain. The gourd lay on its side, its wide opening ringed with guard bees.

"Can I open my eyes?" Ndurumo asked.

Silence.

"Can I open now?"

More silence.

Focused on his discovery and aware it wasn't wise to alert the hive, Njerũ kept quiet.

The bees produced sweet honey, the same kind Baba harvested from his hives. Excited, Njerũ longed to gather honey and surprise his brothers.

"You're taking too long," Ndurumo called.

Njerũ held his peace, still debating how Baba harvested honey.

He climbed out of the granary in search of a tool.

Ndurumo opened his eyes when he heard Njerũ walk about. "You don't want me to find you?"

"Wait," Njerũ said. "I'll show you." He scavenged around the courtyard. At the fence, he broke the straightest twig he could find and returned to the gourd.

He inserted the stick gently to avoid disturbing the bees. When the stick hit something solid, he twisted it and pulled it out; a dab of honey glistened on its tip.

Before he dipped again, the bees had mobilized. They cleared the gourd's opening in a cloud, buzzing and flying in all directions.

Njerŭ dropped the stick and scrambled for the exit, tripping over bags and tools, hollering as he flailed his arms. The lead bees swarmed after him. As he reached the door, he thrust his leg out. Before his foot landed on the stepping board, he half tumbled to the ground, the mob of bees right behind him.

Ndurumo and Machira took off, burst into nyŭmba, and shut the door. The two grown-ups behind the homestead did the same. Bees flooded into the courtyard.

Confused and terrified, it never occurred to Njerŭ to follow his brothers. He hollered and ran toward the main entrance on the footpath leading away from home; the bees trailing in a tight, angry formation.

*

Waigwa, my half-brother in his early twenties, was walking home from work. From a distance, he saw bees circling a spot like an animated mound. As he approached, he heard faint whimpering and noticed streaks of clothing beneath the swarm. He removed his coat, swatted frantically, ducked through the stingers, scooped Njerŭ, and covered his head as he rushed him to safety.

When Mother arrived home and saw her son, she let out a piercing scream. Every inch of his body was swollen. His tongue stuck out, too big for his mouth. His cries had dwindled to grunts.

Mother washed and plucked every stinger she could find. She and Baba started another round of home remedies—herbs, ointments, and daily washes with Baba's homemade beer. After each wash, she gave him a sip or two.

Nobody expected Njerũ to survive his second ordeal either. But once again, he surprised everyone when death gave him another chance.

From that day, no matter what Waigwa did, Mother reserved a soft spot in her heart for him for saving her son.

7. Ndurumo

Trouble in our home did not choose just one child. If Njerũ seemed marked by near-disasters, Ndurumo had his own brushes with harm, sudden but just as startling.

Mother heard yells from the courtyard and rushed outside in full defense mode, only to find the aggressor and victim were her own children.

Njerũ, wide-eyed, stood frozen. Ndurumo bent forward, his arms limp at his sides, while one of his eyeballs dangled on his cheekbone. He screamed, shaking as if his eyeball preyed on him.

Mother rushed him indoors. She examined him and, ever so carefully, repositioned the bloody blob. She soothed him while she cleaned his eye and face.

"What happened?" she asked when Ndurumo could speak.

"Njerũ poked me."

"It's not me; it's the thorn," Njerũ said from the doorway.

When things calmed down, Mother and Baba weighed the matter. They agreed there had been no malice between their two sons. The boys were playing, they said. It was just an accident.

Within two weeks, the swelling subsided. Besides slight sensitivity, the eye looked almost normal when Mother touched it to check. Neither Ndurumo nor anyone else realized he now had a damaged left eye.

Life resumed its rhythm. No one paid attention as the injured eye slowly shifted into a new shade of auburn with a blue center, unlike his other deep navy-blue eye.

I didn't notice Ndurumo had two different eyes until my teens, when I overheard Mother talking with another woman about the trials of raising children.

"It's hard to keep an eye on them every waking moment," she said. "My oldest poked his brother's eye while I was right there at home."

"That's why he has a njata—a star?" the woman asked.

"Yes."

Except for that brief exchange, none of us—siblings or parents—mentioned the eye. The silence surrounding it became its own kind of our family's truth, among the things we never talked about.

As an adult, I longed to ask Ndurumo what he remembered, his side of the story. I wanted to know whether the eye could see, and whether it grieved him. But I never gathered the courage.

Even younger relatives never asked him when they noticed. But they always associated him with the eye in his absence. If I mentioned him to those unfamiliar with him, a voice always chimed in, "Is it the uncle with njata in the eye?"

"Yes," I would say, and leave it at that.

Decades later, when I visited Ndurumo in June 2016, I noticed his eyes looked the same. That gave me the courage to pry.

"Did you do something to your eyes?" I asked. "They look so clear."

"I consulted an eye doctor," he said.

"You did?"

"Yes. He fixed it."

"Oh, that's great." It never occurred to me to ask *how*.

"The doctor said if I had gone to the hospital when it happened, they would have saved my eye."

Ndurumo said this with quiet regret. It touched me deeply. I hesitated before gathering the courage to ask him one more critical question, hoping against hope that the answer would be yes. "Does the eye see?"

"No."

"Oh," I said, and fell silent.

He shrugged lightly before he said, "Children get into all sorts of accidents before they grow up." He retold the thorn story, almost casually, as if it were an old fable. When he finished, I wanted more answers, like:

When did he realize he was blind in that eye?

Did it hurt him when he found out?

As an adult, did he feel resentment toward Njerũ?

But courage failed me. Besides, I did not want to plant a negative seed about something I believed, perhaps hoped, had never bothered him before.

To my relief, Ndurumo shifted the conversation to a different childhood incident, one I had heard as a young girl.

*

Before I was born, Baba owned two donkeys: Toto and the one I'll call Punda. Along the way, Punda gave birth to Njeremani; whose paternal parentage I never learned. The three donkeys were not only beasts of burden, but none of their stories ended well. Punda faded from the family's memory; nobody seemed to know what happened to her, and Baba wasn't talking. Bees attacked Njeremani, and after an agonizing period, it died from the stings. But Toto had a spectacular experience before Baba forced it out of the family.

One afternoon, while the children played in the courtyard, Njerũ rushed Toto the way I later saw my brothers dash toward a goat for fun. Not interested in Njerũ's kind of mischief, Toto snapped out a kick.

Usually, the boys ducked, laughed, and backed away. But this time, Njerũ did not duck fast enough. Toto's kick landed and knocked him to the ground. Frightened and in pain, Njeru hollered. But Toto was not done. It turned, raised its right hoof, and brought it down on Njerũ's cheek. A series of screams followed in quick succession.

Mother ran outdoors to save her child yet again. When she poured water into Njerũ's mouth to clean the blood, it gushed out through the cheek. The hoof had landed when Njerũ's mouth was wide open in a scream.

After another home-healing regimen, Njerũ survived, though he kept a half-moon scar on his cheek, a signature of Toto's bad temper.

Poor Toto was prone to sudden anger. He snapped, kicked, and walked away without looking back. But that day, he crossed a line, and he paid dearly for it.

Baba pierced the offending leg with a spear and beat the poor animal with sticks until he got tired. He then disowned the donkey. Toto took a long while to recover before anyone agreed to buy him.

Those childhood traumas—abandonment, mystery illness, the bees, the donkey—all happened before Njerũ started school. And before Aunt Julia, Baba's youngest sister, stepped in with her own well-intentioned authority, which brought Njerũ yet another stretch of hardship.

8. The Dare

By the time Ndurumo suffered irreparable harm to his eye, and Njerũ survived bees and donkeys, one truth had become clear in our family: whatever hardship did not find a child by chance would find them because of our place of birth or by tradition. Sometimes, it arrived not through misfortune but through the will of another person. In Njerũ's case, that person was Aunt Julia.

She visited my family when I was a year old. She was disappointed to learn that Njerũ had not started school. When she spoke to Baba about it, he said he wanted the nine-year-old to get older. According to him, Njerũ was not old or strong enough to tackle a one-way five- or six-mile walk across the savanna and over Jumatatu Mountain range to the one-room school at Gathĩrĩga Primary School at Ndege's farm.

Aunt Julia did not care for excuses. She fussed about Njerũ needing to attend school without further delay. Unlike my parents, she had gone to school through her own determination.

Following her mother's death when she was six years old, her father, who had only married her widowed mother in hopes of a son, had abandoned Aunt Julia. After a horrific period of struggle, she and her three half-siblings finally pulled through.

As a tween, Aunt Julia learned that Tũmũtũmũ Missionary Boarding School was scouting for orphaned girls or girls whose fathers would permit them to attend. She saw her chance to get an education. She defied Baba, her older brother by thirteen years, slipped from his grip, and ran all the way to the missionary boarding school. Her pursuing brother gave up and turned around when Aunt Julia shot into the school building like an arrow, huffing and panting.

Aunt Julia became one of the "Mambare," the first five girls to attend school in Nyeri County. She ended up better informed and financially secure even before she retired from her nursing job. So, my parents respected her and went along with most of her suggestions.

She had intervened a year earlier, when she visited along with her boyfriend, Ishmael, and took Gĩthũi-big, the last son of Baba's first family. He started school in Mũrang'a, where he lived with Ishmael Gĩchũhĩ's family, and would remain until he completed eighth grade.

Now, at the end of her visit, she took Njerũ as well. She enrolled him in a school near Nyeri General Hospital, where she worked. After a year of non-goat-herding, a better diet, and a cleaner environment, Njerũ thrived into a healthy, vibrant boy.

But his life was about to change. His living with Aunt Julia in a hospital-provided single room interfered with her personal and work schedule. She also decided he needed company because he arrived home from school before she got off work.

She, already married and divorced, had established her home on a piece of land she had bought in Irũri, Gataka-inĩ, and built an L-shaped house. She stayed there during her annual leave or on her days off.

Njerũ-big, Baba's first son, lived there with his wife, Njoki, daughter of Gathuya, and their three-year-old son, Mwangi. They minded the land and livestock and kept Aunt Julia's home maintained.

When she considered her living arrangement, she decided that a change would not only improve her social life but also give Njerũ a family life.

She took him to her home, registered him at Kanyota Primary School, and left him in the care of Njerũ-big and his wife.

Months later, back in Solai, Baba heard of an outbreak of hunger in Nyeri known as Ng'aragu ya Gathũa. But my parents believed Njerũ lived with Aunt Julia. And because she did not live off her land, where a dry spell could devastate her livelihood, they did not fret about their son's well-being.

But on his way home one day, Baba met a man who had recently visited Nyeri. The man told Baba how hunger had devastated the entire Nyeri.

"When I saw your boy," the man said, "I failed to understand why you let him remain there."

"He looked that bad?"

"Only an orphan would look like that."

"Are you sure it was my boy?" Baba was still doubtful.

"Of course, it was your son," the man said. "I stopped by your sister's, but she wasn't there."

Back home, Baba and Mother still doubted the man's story. But within three months, Baba received a letter from Aunt Julia confirming that Njerũ now lived with Njerũ-big's family.

*

Njerũ-big, the first son of the Warama family and namesake of Baba's father, never got along with his own father. Friction between the two began when he resisted Baba's cruelty and poor treatment, or fought back.

According to his sister Gathoni—now the only one alive who witnessed what happened—the father-and-son relationship reached a breaking point one Sunday afternoon in 1945, when Baba and Kaguyu, their mother, hosted a small drinking party for a handful of close friends. The guests left in the late afternoon, except for two men who lounged outside.

Drunk, Baba returned to his thingira. Not long after, he went back to Kaguyu's house, where she sat with her two married sons, Njerũ-big and Waigwa. For reasons Gathoni never fully understood—perhaps an old grievance, or suspicion that they were colluding against him—Baba began assaulting them with a whip. The family had endured his cruelty for years and was worn down by it.

Seeing his mother cry out, Njerũ-big could not take it anymore. He shot out of the house and rummaged for a good-sized stick at the edge of the courtyard, ready for battle.

Stick in hand, he marched toward his mother's house, breathing hard and muttering, "No one will beat me alongside my mother." To his frustration, the two men in the courtyard grabbed and restrained him.

"There won't be any more fighting today," one of them said.

Meanwhile, Baba slipped away and returned to his thingira.

To cool his fury, Njerũ-big turned to the back of the homestead where young maize plants grew. He swung the stick with all the energy he could muster and cleared half the garden, as a scythe would.

The following morning, he left Kĩrĩma-inĩ in a huff and swore he would never live in Baba's homestead again.

And now, Aunt Julia, without checking with Baba, appointed the same Njerũ-big and his allegedly lazy wife as the guardians of Njerũ-little, born of a wife who had allegedly edged his mother out of the limelight in the Warama household, sentiments that his sister Gathoni shared with me decades later.

*

Back then, Baba did not reply to Aunt Julia's letter. Instead, he took a Saturday off and traveled to Nyeri—an entire day's safari in those days. When he knocked on Njerũ-big's door, he and his wife were so surprised they thought somebody had died.

Baba had not returned to Nyeri for a long, long time.

"No, everyone is okay in Solai," Baba said. "I heard people are dying of hunger here."

"We are getting by," Njerũ-big said.

Later, after a supper of sweet potatoes, a third of a normal portion, Njoki prepared a plank bed in the wooden cottage next to Aunt Julia's house. Baba, Njerũ, and little Mwangi left to spend the night in the cottage.

When all went quiet, Baba dug in his bag and produced a whole, cooked, fatty goat's head. He unwrapped it and, with his pocketknife, carved slices of meat. He and the boys ate their fill, and Baba returned the clean skull to his bag to discard later.

"Njerũ, Njerũ, wake up," Baba said softly, shaking Njerũ at dawn.

"Aaah…"

"Get up. Get up. We are going home."

"Our home?"

Before Baba confirmed, Njerũ had shot up, scrambled for his clothes, and followed, leaving his exercise books behind.

He remained in the courtyard while Baba knocked at the big house.

"I'm taking Njerũ-little with me," Baba said when Njerũ-big came to the door.

"I thought you would stay for a few days."

"No. I need to get back to work."

"You don't have to take him; we are getting by."

"I think it'll be easier for your family without him."

*

When Baba and his now almost eleven-year-old son neared Kĩrĩma-inĩ, and Njerũ recognized our homestead, he quickened his shuffle, rounded the fence, and reached the entrance ahead of Baba. Mother, seated on her porch shelling beans, stopped to observe the little boy in a well-worn shirt, shorts, and a little jacket. The shoes Aunt Julia had bought him had fallen apart and were long gone. He swayed side-to-side as if every step he took tortured him. But the boy grinned, swinging his arms.

What a strange child! Mother thought, as she said later.

Meanwhile, Baba appeared at the entrance.

In a second, Mother shrieked. She dumped the tray; half the beans scattered across the ground as she rushed to meet her son. "Oh! Mwana wakwa!" (Oh! My child!), Mother said. "Nĩmanyonjeria mwana!" They have maimed my child!

Surprised by Mother's reaction, Njerũ froze.

When she reached him, she inspected him from head to his feet, all the while talking to herself as only a mother could, without seeming nutty.

Various jigger clusters littered his feet—between his toes, on toe-tips, under his toenails, on his heels, and on the sides. His soles were the only parts of his feet that remained uninfected. His hands and even his elbows displayed a cluster of little bumps.

Mother used a safety pin to dig out and remove the jiggers. She started with the fattest little white balls, which she removed in stages so as not to leave too many gaping wounds. She then washed the sores with Dettol amid Njerũ's winces.

In about a week, she cleared flea larvae from his body. While his sores healed, she fed him as if he had a disability.

As Baba did when Mother gave birth, he slaughtered a goat so Njerũ could feed on herbal-spiced soups. It took him more than a month to recover from a year's neglect and starvation.

I never heard whether Aunt Julia saw Njerũ in that state. If she did, shame on her. But when she learned that Baba had taken Njerũ back to Solai, she wrote him a scathing letter, accusing him of preferring his children to remain illiterate.

"Now that you have withdrawn Njerũ-little from school," she accused. "We'll see whether you can afford to educate him."

Baba did not reply to his sister's letter or address the subject again. But deep inside him, I do not doubt it was game on.

My family told and retold the dare story so many times that every family member alive had heard it—or, if unborn, would hear it when they arrived.

9. Dare's Challenges

According to Waigwa, when he read Aunt Julia's letter to Baba, and reached the part where she said, "We'll see whether you can afford to educate Njerŭ-little," Baba had scoffed and made slow nods. After Waigwa finished reading, Baba had tucked the letter into his shirt pocket without a word. But the barb had struck its target. How dare she? He may have asked himself.

From then on, Njerŭ became a tool for Baba to prove his ability or lack thereof. Based on Baba and his sister's stances, whether Njerŭ learned or remained illiterate depended less on his ability and more on who won the dare. Neither seemed to consider what that meant for the child caught between them.

*

After Njerŭ regained his health at eleven, Baba made his move. He took time off from work and braved Jumatatu Mountain Range to the one-room Gathĩrĩga Primary School. The headmaster agreed that Njerŭ could join Grade Two. Five or six miles of savanna and one mountain range or not, Njerŭ would go to school.

He walked to school alone because the only other schoolboy in our area lived about three miles east of his way. Mother worried about her son's safety, but she kept it to herself. She woke him early, fed him porridge, packed his lunch in a small kĩondo, and sent him off.

Njerũ accepted the distance; what choice did he have? But he worried about the horde of goatboys who ambushed and bullied him on his way home. After he descended the slope of Jumatatu Mountain, he found them engaged in their escapades while their herds grazed nearby in the savanna. They taunted, jeered, and called him a softie before devising a way to entrap him. They refused to let him pass unless he boxed the youngest boy in their group.

The first time, Njerũ felt confident. His opponent looked small enough. The boys formed a circle; the two boxers proceeded to the center; the referee flapped his hand, and the match began. After a few jabs amidst a chorus of hoots and jeers, Njerũ knocked the boy down.

"That's not fair!" the spectators protested.

A compromise followed without Njeru's input: he must also fight the second-youngest. And so it went.

At best, the matches ended in exhaustion. At worst, the boys roughed Njerũ, kicked him, and sent him limping home with a bloody nose he wiped clean before he arrived.

He took part in three impromptu *matches* before the mere sight or voices of his tormentors made him tremble and break into a sprint. But he still suffered taunts and a kick or two from a determined boy who kept up the chase.

When the goatboys' herds grazed at a different part of the savanna, Njerũ caught a break. But they knew when he walked home, so they hung around longer. He thought about dropping out of school. But that would create a bigger problem at home.

Instead, he learned to evade. He scanned the savanna for goat herds before he descended the mountain. If he spotted herds grazing nearby, he slipped through cover like a wary animal and ducked behind thorny bushes until they wandered inland.

As he grew older and wiser, he grew tired of running and avoidance alone felt insufficient. As an emerging teen and a goat-herder on weekends, he understood that sometimes a person needed more than fists or swift feet or even reason to settle a quarrel. He pondered ways of defending himself, and a weapon came to mind.

For an entire week, he shaped a one-and-a-half-foot club with a smooth, knobby end the size of a small orange. He hid it half a mile from school and retrieved it each afternoon. The woods became his practice ground. While he waited for the goatboys to disappear, he perfected his swings.

Only when he felt ready did he signal his new confidence.

From the top of Jumatatu Mountain, overlooking Kamunge's farm, Njerũ called out the names of his brothers. His voice echoed for miles. Ndurumo, herding goats farther inland, answered him. Sometimes Mother, walking home from work or from the garden, heard the calls too.

I once heard the distant echoes of hollers while accompanying Mother to her job. "Those are your brothers making that racket," she said.

Maybe the goatboys suspected he carried a weapon, or he had reinforcements. Whatever the case, they never waited for him again.

Njerũ lamented a waste of his troubles; he hadn't had a chance to crack the club on a tormentor's head, shoulder, or even back. Strapped with limited life experience, he did not yet understand that in harsh rural places, no skill went to waste.

10. Hazards of Boyhood

Njerũ's world was widening in ways none of us understood then. Every day he walked those miles alone—across the savanna, up and down Jumatatu Mountain, past cattle pens and thorny scrub—his body growing stronger, his instincts sharper.

It was a lonely route, yes, but also a learning experience. The dare between Baba and Aunt Julia had set him on that path, but the land itself had taken over his training. What waited for him, however, were tests no child should have had to face alone.

Besides the goatboys who ambushed him, Njerũ soon learned that the savanna held another unpredictable danger: snakes. No child raised on Kamunge's farm grew up without crossing paths with one.

One afternoon on his way home from school, he swung his club absentmindedly as he trudged along the footpath. He came upon a snake lying stretched under a shade at the trail's edge. Startled by his approach, it slithered and vanished into the tall grass. A wiser child might have thanked the heavens and walked on. But after weeks of practicing his club swings, imagining the day he would defend himself against the Toughs, Njerũ felt compelled to test his weapon.

He veered off the path in pursuit.

When the snake became aware of its pursuer, it burst forward in a streak, weaving through grass tufts and shrubs. The boy and the snake turned into hunter and prey.

At last, the snake stopped fleeing. It whipped around, lifted its head, half its length rising off the ground. It hissed, warning him, daring him.

That was enough for Njerũ. Panic surged through him. He spun and raced back toward the path, club still in hand, the grass whipping his legs. When he reached the open trail, he dared a glance over his shoulder.

The snake followed.

Fear shook him. He zigzagged. The snake glided smoothly through the grass, gaining speed. He forced himself to run straight along the dirt path, hoping the rough surface would slow the creature down. But the snake was no fool; it rode the grassy edges, keeping pace.

Njeru's breath tore from his lungs. His heart hammered so fiercely he feared it would burst. In an instant, instinct overtook thought. His body moved on its own.

He pivoted, lifted off the ground, and brought the club down in a single, desperate arc.

By the time his feet landed on the path, the snake's head lay crushed flat. Its body twisted and quivered before stilling altogether.

Decades later, when Njerũ retold the story, he shook his head in disbelief.

"A phenomenon," he said. "Divine intervention."

He never again pursued a snake.

*

But the land had another test in store for Njerũ.

Kamunge's cows drank from concrete troughs scattered at strategic points in the rambling cow pens and grazing fields. The regular troughs measured approximately 10 x 5 feet and were three feet high, with a seven-inch-thick concrete wall on top, on which people could sit and splash water with their feet. But it was against farm rules for anyone to touch that water. Occasionally, however, boys sneaked in for a splash or an illicit swim.

One blazing afternoon, boredom tugged at Njerũ as he walked home. He wandered off the footpath and discovered a trough unlike any he had seen before—massive, ringed by shrubs and a single large tree only feet away, offering shade. The water rippled and shimmered in the gentle breeze, under the equatorial heat, tempting him.

Njerũ wished he could dive in, just once. But he didn't know how to swim. That had been a luxury of boys who lived in clusters of homesteads. They built makeshift dams on the Tindaress River and turned them into their secret playgrounds. He and Ndurumo had grown up too isolated at Kĩrĩma-inĩ to learn from others.

Still, the water tugged at him.

He reasoned that he could hold on to the rim, dip in, splash, and cool off. No one would know. And if he braved it for several days, he might even teach himself how to swim.

He placed his schoolbag and clothes safely out of reach of the water. Naked, crouching low, he approached the trough, ready to hoist himself up.

He sensed a presence. As he raised his head, a flicker caught his eye.

A man's head emerged from behind the nearby tree—slow, deliberate; wide, blank eyes stared.

Njerũ dropped into a squat, hoping the man hadn't seen him. He waited. When he heard no rustling, he raised his eyes level with the water.

The head was gone.

He waited another minute before rising and preparing to try again.

The head reappeared, in slow motion, and a glimpse of a white shirt slid into view. The man's face stayed expressionless; his wide, cautionary eyes steady.

Njerũ ducked again, frustrated but intrigued; he sensed no danger.

He waited longer this time. When all fell still, he crept along to the trough's narrow side. Again, he rose, meaning to jump in quickly. But he couldn't suppress his curiosity. He looked.

The head emerged once more, this time full-chested—slow, sorrowful, pleading, warning him.

Njeru dropped down, trembling, and crept to where he had left his books and clothes. He grabbed them, ran a short distance naked, then dressed in haste before racing all the way home.

*

Months later, with the sun scorching the earth in January, he remembered the trough—the cool water, the missed chance. He decided to try again.

But when he reached the site, the trough was bone-dry.

Confused, he peered over the rim. Only a tiny silver glint shimmered deep below, reflecting like a tiny mirror. I think I made a mistake, he told himself. This can't be it. He took another quick peek to be sure.

He backed away and scanned the landscape. The tree was the same, though nearly leafless now. The memory of the man's pleading eyes washed over him. Fear of what would have happened gripped him.

He rushed away without a second glance.

But secrets feel heavier when shouldered alone. Njerũ's secret gnawed on him. That evening, he dropped a hint as the family gathered around the fire.

"A boy in school said there's a huge trough somewhere on this farm."

Mother nodded. "That's true."

"He said it goes deep into the ground."

"Yes. It's a bottomless pit," Mother said. "Cows used to disappear before they fenced it. Kamunge built a trough around it."

"Where is it?"

"That shouldn't be your concern."

Njerũ fell silent. He never wandered onto that part of the savanna again.

*

During those lonely years, between snakes, the goatboys' ambushes, and bottomless pits disguised as water troughs, Njerũ grew weary of his tedious trek to school and the hassle involved.

One Friday morning, just before he started climbing Jumatatu Mountain, an idea of a long weekend teased him. He slipped into the woods just before he began the climb. He spent the day terrorizing birds and squirrels by pelting them with gravel. Without a schedule, he ate his lunch earlier than usual. In the afternoon, he picked wild blackberries, gooseberries, and other berries. And even squeezed in a nap before heading home, wearing a tired, after-school look.

Because parents never visited their children's schools in those days, Njerũ planned to attend school whenever he chose. He figured his secret was safe.

But Mr. Jacob Rũrĩrĩ, headmaster and lone teacher of the one-room Gathĩrĩga Primary School, had no patience for truants. That Saturday, he walked all the way to Kĩrĩma-inĩ to check on his student.

Njerũ received two whippings: one from Baba and another the following Monday when he reported to school.

With that kind of dedication, my parents spoke of Mr. Rũrĩrĩ with the same admiration often reserved for modern-day celebrities.

After that, Njerũ saw no other refuge but to concentrate on his studies.

His trials, however, were far from over, but each ordeal toughened the boy who had once been called Softie. What none of us knew then was that the next test waiting for him came not from the land or its creatures, but from within our own family.

11. Steamed Maize

Njerũ's ordeals: bullies, snakes, mysterious troughs, the long, lonely march toward education, and potential ones stood in sharp contrast to the quieter world I inhabited in those early years. While his life unfolded in the savanna and at school, mine pulsed inside the boundaries of the homestead, beside Mother's skirts, under Baba's shadow, and within the rhythms of chores by others.

As I approached age six, Mother decided it was time I shouldered small responsibilities—duties she had once pressed onto my older brothers, and which she now hoped I, her first daughter, would carry with grace.

I should mention that I came along after five boys—two gone and three alive. My sister Nyandia followed two years later. Before we girls arrived, Mother had already trained Njerũ and Ndurumo to help with certain "female" chores such as babysitting and carrying loads on their backs. My brothers had not yet frowned on such tasks because Baba did not interfere, and no boys lived close enough to tease or shame them. But once Nyandia and I entered the picture, Mother found new satisfaction. In a few years, her daughters would finally ease her burden of women's work.

She began training me about a month or two before I turned six. She singled me out for a trip to our garden. I felt important, chosen for a mission that marked my growing up. Before that day, I doubt I had ever walked over twenty yards outside our homestead unless someone strapped me on their back.

In the garden, Mother weeded and plucked green vegetables. Before packing them, she rose with one hand on her hip, surveyed the spread of greenery, and shook her head. "This maize should be ready by now," she said.

I looked up, confused. "It's big," I said, stretching my arm toward an ear I couldn't reach.

"Yes, it's taller than you," she said, "but it's not ready for us to eat."

We packed and left when Mother placed the smaller kĩondo of vegetables inside the larger empty one, covered the light load with an empty sack, and hoisted it onto her back. On the footpath home, we joined a broader tractor trail running beside a massive, green maize plantation stretching for acres. Mother paused and eyed the towering plants. "This maize is ready," she said.

Then why did she say ours was not ready? I asked myself.

A few steps later, she stopped abruptly. I nearly bumped into her behind. "My children should be eating maize this time of year," she said.

I waited, wondering.

She scanned the open savanna—front, back, left, right— then dashed straight into the plantation. "Come," she called.

I plunged in behind her without a word, unaware of what she was up to. I tripped on weeds, slipped in soft soil, and swiped hairy leaves away from my face and arms. My exposed skin itched. Mother moved quickly, only slowing when she lost sight of me.

"Are you still coming? Are you all right?"

Sometimes I forgot to answer, too busy dodging leaves. She walked mere steps ahead, where I could see parts of her dress, yet she seemed so far away.

The deeper we went, the dimmer the light became, and soon the earth smelled cool and fresh, unlike anything I had known.

Finally, we reached a place where the soil looked dark and rich, where only thin weeds survived under the maize canopy. Mother lowered her load, separated the kĩondo from the vegetables, and set it beside me. "Wait here," she said, and slung the empty big kĩondo's strap across her chest.

Then she went on the offensive. She examined each ear, feeling, judging. Some she left. Others she snapped off cleanly, slipping them tip-first into the large kĩondo. She moved fast, jumping around, never stripping two plants in a row, and only one ear from a plant, restoring leaves to conceal what she had taken. Then she vanished between rows. When she reappeared, her kĩondo bulged. She set it down and rearranged the maize ears.

"I'll be back," she said before dashing off again.

Not enough, I thought.

She reappeared with an armful of maize. After she stuck and rearranged them, she hurried off again for her last haul. When kĩondo could hold no more, she covered it tightly with the empty sack, hoisted it onto her back, and placed the smaller vegetable kĩondo on top.

"Let's go," she said.

We emerged from the plantation far from where we had entered. Another glance around—front, back, across the open land—and she stepped onto the trail toward home, steady as if the detour never happened. I trotted close behind.

At home, Mother set the maize aside and started on her evening chores. When the house quieted at dusk, and Baba sipped his mug of tea, she husked the ears, leaving thin layers intact. She layered them in the pot, added the loose husks on top, poured water, covered it with an iron lid, and set the pot over the fire.

When the cooked maize appeared on our white enamel plates, we filled the house with loud, unrestrained chatter, excited to eat the juicy, sweet first maize of the season.

"Shhh," Mother hissed.

We turned toward her.

She jerked her chin toward thingira.

We clamped our mouths before we resumed our chatter in low voices.

My brothers exchanged puzzled glances—silence was not typical during supper.

For me, the truth became obvious. From the detour into the plantation to the muted excitement now, the pieces fell into place: Mother had taken maize from someone else's garden, and we must not let Baba know.

She confirmed this when she served him supper without maize.

Today, I wonder what might have happened had Kamunge's workers caught my mother. Theft on a colonial farm meant fines, beatings, and even a criminal record.

For Kamunge, I believe he would have deducted his estimate of the maize's value from Baba's wages. In addition, he would have rebuked Baba for "failing to control his wife," a humiliation that cut deeply during colonial times. British farmers threw such rebukes at African men to belittle or to show them how powerless they were, even in their own homes. (It has always been important to an African man, especially during the colonial era, that if he could not manage anything else, he could at least manage his own homestead.)

Such rebukes, or the mere thought of them, turned some men into family brutes.

However, if Baba alone had discovered her theft, Mother might have faced only the bullwhip.

But I was the sole witness, a witness she must have believed too young to understand. For her sake, I never shared it with a soul. Even at six, I understood something about loyalty. Children did not cross or betray their parents. I kept the secret through childhood and adulthood, never sharing it, even when we later revealed childhood secrets and mischief. I did not want to embarrass my mother, especially because, as we grew older, she became as strict about theft as my father.

Years later, I understood why our maize lagged. Kamunge got his own vast plantations plowed and planted first. Only afterward did he send the tractor to prepare the small plots he allotted to his African workers. He then gave women laborers time off to prepare and plant their gardens.

And it took even longer to understand that Kamunge did not plow employees' plots out of kindness.

12. My First Job

Not long after the maize incident, our household slipped into a different rhythm, one I did not yet understand.

Instead of finding Mother doing her morning chores, I awoke and found two women in our house. One woman remained in Mother's bedroom, which made me conclude she had overslept and was being woken. The second woman busied herself by the fire, cooking our porridge and Baba's tea. After our breakfast, the woman insisted that we, the children, play outside.

Deep in our activities, we heard a baby's cries. Confused, I wondered what to make of it. We had no baby in our house; the youngest was among us.

"Is it my brother Macharia who has come?" Baba asked from the courtyard.

Mother, exhausted, needed to catch her breath. The two women didn't yet know who the baby would be named after. So, no sound came from Mother's bedroom for a long pause.

"Yes," the two women answered in unison.

"That's good news," Baba said. "Our Kĩbinga has arrived."

It so happened that Baba's brother had been named after his uncle Kĩbinga, an industrious man who searched relentlessly for whatever he had his eye on. People began calling him Macharia, meaning "one who searches." By the time Baba's brother was born, the name Macharia had stuck.

My mother later said she was surprised that Baba had correctly guessed the baby's gender.

With that one question and answer, the baby's name became Macharia.

Mother said nothing afterward. She could not tell whether Baba had mixed the names or done it intentionally. Whatever the case, she could do nothing to undo Baba's pronouncement or fuss about her newborn's name. Besides, Agĩkũyũ did not transfer namesakes.

According to our custom, parents alternate naming their children between the husband's and the wife's families. The rule fails only if the new parents had fallen out of favor with the would-be-named-after candidate. He or she might state that they should never be named in that family. In that case, the next in line assumes the honor.

Other instances are when a wife strays and sneaks a baby into the family, or an out-of-wedlock birth (and the man doesn't hold his end of the bargain). Such children are always named after the mother's relatives.

In my family's case, my parents had already named my two-year-old brother Gĩthũi after Baba's brother. (Decades later, I learned this was a replacement name—the boy born after Ndurumo had also been named after Baba's brother and had died as a toddler.) Ordinarily, the next boy should have been named after Mother's brother. With five boys alive, this would have meant three named after Mother's side and only two after Baba's. I doubt Baba wanted such a setup.

The following day, Mother emerged from her bedroom holding the baby swaddled in a brand-new towel. He smelled raw and new, like strange milk, his head covered in slick, curly jet-black hair. His face and the tiny, uncovered hands looked fragile, as if they were skinless. I stared at him as if someone had set an oddity among us.

My curiosity faded as his body slowly toughened into skin like ours, and Mother snipped away his slippery womb hair, as she called it.

Chũchũ Nyandia, my maternal grandmother, after whom Nyandia, my sister, is named, came to see the baby, the only time I met any of my grandparents.

She wore a skirt with tiny prints under a light brown dress, clipped together with safety pins at the shoulder and from the right armpit to the knee. Her earlobes dangled with no earrings. Seated by the fire, she looked and dressed just like my mother.

The following day or two, before she left, I overheard her tell Mother that she and her husband, Ndurumo, would move to Nyeri, the native reserve. Chũchũ said she wanted to stay, but her husband preferred to leave. He believed the turmoil would get worse for those left on European farms. As we learned much later, he had failed to tell his wife that the landowner had let him go.

I had not yet heard my parents mention such a thing. But that was adult talk that had nothing to do with us children.

Three weeks after she left, my mother returned to work. It was the beginning of November, the height of the coffee cherry-picking season, when the farm owner required everyone to report to work. It was also the period before Christmas, the only public holiday, when casual workers earned more money than usual.

With a one-month-old baby, too young for Mother to strap on her back while she picked coffee, she needed a babysitter. But she had few options.

Njerũ, the oldest, attended school the entire day. The second son, Ndurumo, herded goats in the mornings and left to attend grade one in the afternoons. He left his eight-year-old brother, Machira, to mind the goats alone.

As the next in line, at six years old, Mother gave me the babysitting job, a role I would later find myself stuck with in the village as if it were my childhood career.

Mother and I walked three miles to the coffee plantation where the employer had directed people to report for work. She carried Macharia sideways across her chest in a sheet of cloth that she draped and tied over her shoulders like a sling. I was excited to accompany Mother to her job for the first time, and I don't remember getting tired. But I recall her strolling and talking to me.

We had taken so long that when we arrived, we found people already picking coffee cherries. I marveled at the sight of rows and rows of young coffee bushes. The highest stood about six feet tall with branches filled with clusters of red coffee cherries. Back then, I had not developed a concept of beauty or seen fruit trees, so I did not realize the plantation looked like a vineyard, with bushes bursting with red grapes before harvest.

When Mother got to her row, she fetched a fresh sheet of cloth from her kĩondo and spread it under a shady coffee bush. She laid Macharia down and told me to sit and watch him.

Whenever she progressed and lost sight of us, she moved us to a bush closer to her.

She took breaks several times to suckle Macharia.

At lunchtime, she and I ate gĩtheri, a mixture of maize, beans, potatoes, and vegetables, and drank water from a gourd.

"It's better to use a gourd," she said. "It keeps water cool longer than a bottle."

Because of boredom, sleep often weighed on my eyes. I nodded this way and that, and other times I dropped beside Macharia and slept.

"Oh, the lookout slept," Mother said when she came to move us, and I stirred and opened my eyes.

Macharia's belly button healed and firmed when he was still light enough for me to carry on my back. I was six and a half years old the first time Mother put him on my back. That was during our last move from Kĩrĩma-inĩ. I carried him in a ngoi, the traditional Gĩkũyũ baby carrier, with the strap across my head. To prevent him from tumbling down, if my head jerked backward, Mother reinforced the ngoi with a sheet of cloth knotted across my chest.

Traditionally, Agĩkũyũ made ngoi from cured leather. But by the time I carried Macharia in the 1950s, Mother used store-bought ngoi made from desert green canvas. Later, when I resumed carrying him at the village, my mother upgraded to a tailor-made ngoi made from heavy khaki material. She dubbed it modern and as durable as canvas.

In time, like traditional homesteads with courtyards, ngoi disappeared. If someone wanted one, I doubt any remain in Kenya.

Nowadays, mothers carry babies in their arms, or older babies latch astride their mothers' or carriers' hips. On long distances, mothers tie babies to their backs with pieces of cloth. But ngoi is alive and well elsewhere.

In California, United States, a person only needs to stroll around on pleasant days, especially in summer, to see men and women carrying their offspring in ngoi replicas, now with straps across the carrier's back or chest.

Someone in the West is likely to have been credited with "inventing" ngoi centuries after Gĩkũyũ mothers.

13. Work Perks

To an outsider, accompanying my mother to her job to babysit my little brother might have looked like a duty, a burden on a six-year-old. But to me, it was an honor. I enjoyed having her to myself. Despite having little to tell her, she spoke to me as if she were talking to a colleague. Baby Macharia was no competition; he slept most of the time and rarely cried. I also enjoyed listening to the stories women shared, sometimes shouting across several rows of coffee bushes.

Some women sang while others, mainly mothers with young children, concentrated on their work to make up for feeding interruptions.

Women outnumbered men about three to one. Most men were young—few of them sons of the full-time workers, and the rest were seasonal workers brought by the farm owner. Although men occasionally commented, I never heard them engage in long-winded conversations as women did. Sometimes, when women caused a racket telling stories or babies' cries disturbed the peace, I heard a hasty comment from a man: "These women!"

Some mothers carried babies on their backs; others brought their budding coffee cherry-picker trainees, my age or older, who carried along little pails and picked from branches closer to the ground.

I never felt lonely, but sometimes I became weary of grown-up talk and activity all day long. Being surrounded by tall green bushes with little else to see dulled my mind. At such times, I longed to play with my sister, Nyandia. But I kept my thoughts to myself.

When we arrived in the morning, we found Baba had already assigned rows of coffee bushes to the pickers. Because we arrived last, Mother didn't wait for him; she merely walked to the next row. From time to time during the day, I heard him speak as he walked about.

At lunchtime, he came to get his lunch from Mother. She carried his food in a small kĩondo when they worked at the same plantation. But most days, Baba carried his own lunch wherever his work took him.

Late afternoon, he told the pickers to stop for the day. "Time is up," he said. "It's time to go." Some of them trailed behind to grab one more fistful. He shooed them away like he did goats at home.

"You've got to go now!" he said, checking along the rows of coffee bushes.

People referred to Baba as nyabaara, overseer (nyapara in Kiswahili), a position he held until my early adulthood. I didn't quite grasp what he did until a year after we moved to the village.

At the coffee factory, people staked their spots on the grassy lot. Mother chose a prime spot close to the receptacle.

"Who wants to walk far carrying a tin full of coffee?" she said.

The sprawl resembled an open-air market or a swap meet, which Kenyans now call Jua Kali (hot sun), where low-income sole proprietors labor under the scorching sun.

People caused various commotions before they settled. They walked about, scouting for ideal spots; women called their stray children; babies cried; and the five-gallon tins clanked as each picker took one from a cluster near the receptacle.

When people settled in their spots, they spread sacks on the ground, poured pyramids of coffee cherries at one end, and sat at the other. They then picked leaves or unripe cherries. Pickers lost half a tin of ripe cherries or a full tin if the unripe ones were excessive. They paid no penalty if the unripe cherries were negligible, as most were. They put those in a sack placed near the receptacle platform.

When pickers became satisfied their coffee would pass the overseer's scrutiny, they filled their tins and carried them to the receptacle. Men held their loads high on their shoulders, and women hugged theirs against their bodies. They passed by Baba, who stood by the platform. The receptacle was a sloping concrete structure, about fifteen feet in diameter and four feet from the ground. At the top, it rounded in front and tapered gradually toward the back, ending in a narrow opening at the lowest point.

This initial inspection ensured that the pickers had not tampered with the tins. To stretch pickings, sometimes a picker pressed in the four sides of a tin or skimped on the topping where cherries needed to pyramid. (Years later, the farm owner ordered that the cherries be levelled at the rims for easier monitoring.) If the overseer noticed the sides of a tin pressed inward or coffee not topped as required, he rejected the coffee. The picker had to return to their spot and correct the infraction before their coffee passed inspection.

But if the overseer caught a picker with unripe coffee cherries commingled with ripe ones inside the tin—invisible until poured—the penalty came fast, with no appeal. With the overseer's mere declaration, the picker lost the whole tin of coffee. Only gamblers took such chances, especially when it got too busy.

When one poured coffee cherries, and it turned out okay, as most did, a picker progressed to the payment stage, where Kamunge threw a shilling into the empty tin. (Leah, my sister-in-law, swears it was fifty cents.)

Meanwhile, two barefoot men, trousers hitched up to their knees, as I later saw men do when they wanted to wade into a river, stood on the receptacle's surface, wielding massive brushes occasionally coaxing laggard cherries along, making sure no cluster dared to back up while they cascaded down to the bottom and disappeared into the factory's bowels.

As I later learned when I became part of the coffee-cherry pickers at the back of the factory, the transformation seemed like a secret revealed. The reddish berries emerged skinless, beige, sticky, with a sweet, translucent syrup, and split in half, like unroasted coffee beans. The beans then proceeded to a wide, three-foot-high tank, like a swirling whirlpool, where the water hissed and churned, scrubbing their sticky bodies bare and spitting them out, ready for factory workers to sun-dry them on raised flatbeds outside.

*

On our way home, the distance seemed longer than in the morning. Tired, I labored to keep up with my mother. She slowed her steps, but no matter how slowly she walked, I often could not keep up with her, especially when I frolicked if I got attracted by a plant, ran my hand through the tall wiregrass, or walked zigzag. She waited for me now and then.

"We would walk all night if you led and set the pace," she said.

That would scare me if it got dark because of my slowness, I thought.

"It's better if an adult leads," she said, "to clear the footpath."

I felt safe and cared for when she said that.

*

Even after Macharia's belly button healed, Mother still carried him on her front. On her back, she carried her coffee-picking paraphernalia or a kĩondo with maize and vegetables she picked if we passed by our garden. By then, our maize was ready. She covered the kĩondo with the now-empty coffee gunnysacks.

Through the savanna, we walked on a narrow footpath with wiregrass and scrub on both sides. With Mother ahead of me, she blocked my view. But I did not realize the disadvantage because my life revolved around her. Besides, I could see beyond her through one side, where the footpath widened. It gave me a measure of freedom to flex my little body because I did not have to walk in a straight line.

One day, it started raining as we crossed the savanna. It quickly got so heavy raindrops dripped down my face; I could not wipe them fast enough to see better. Soon, the wire-grass collapsed and flattened in the narrow parts of the footpath. Whenever I came by such a spot, my six-year-old feet could not sweep through the soaked, heavy grass. I raised my legs higher and stepped on top. I struggled and faltered with every step.

To make it worse, a scatter of little and marble-sized, furious hailstones started falling. I had never seen hailstones rain before, or maybe I had and had forgotten. With my dress already soaked, I walked like a ragdoll, ducking the hail that bounced off my head. It hurt. I covered my head with my hands. That gave me no relief.

Mother turned back and waited. "This rain is too heavy for you," she said.

That seemed obvious to me.

When I reached her, I stepped aside and continued walking, surprised she wanted me to lead, and then, "We would take all night long to get home."

She reached out and said, "Wait," as she pulled me by the shoulder and nuzzled me in front of her.

I turned and looked up at my mother, unsure whether she wanted us to wait for the rain to ebb while she shielded me.

She hurriedly removed two empty gunnysacks from the top of the kiondo on her back. "This rain is too heavy for you," she said.

She said that a few steps ago. What did she want me to do? I wondered.

"I'll have to carry you."

Wow! What a treat! It caught me by surprise. I never expected Mother to carry me like a baby.

I raised my arms, the only time I recall doing so. She always had too many hands raised toward her. Besides the baby, who else could she give such attention to? I had my chance, and I grabbed it.

"You don't have to raise your arms," Mother said, then turned me around. From my back, she clasped her hands under my armpits and lifted me. She could not do it fast enough. By then, the hailstones littered the footpath.

Mother deposited me on top of the kĩondo and nudged me into position. My legs straddled her body around her ribcage, while my chin rested close to her collarbone. Satisfied, she covered me with the empty sacks.

The heavy rain and hailstones pelted my back, making rhythmic sounds like a lullaby. Soothed, I fell asleep within minutes. I woke up when she unloaded me at home. The front of my dress crumpled up, but my body feeling all toasty.

I formed a lifelong happy memory of nurturing warmth and well-being. If I could choose one of my best childhood memories, I would recall that incident with special fondness for my mother.

Family, Marriages & Abuse

14. Polygamy

To understand the household I was born into, one must also understand the social system that shaped marriage, family, and power among the Gĩkũyũ.

One legend claims the Gĩkũyũ nation began as a matriarchal system, when women ruled the land and fought wars like the Dahomey Amazons. (Dahomey was a precolonial West African kingdom in present-day Benin.) The community practiced polyandry—a woman could marry multiple husbands at the same time.

According to the legend, women rulers applied harsh, authoritarian rules that included severe penalties and even capital punishment for philanderers.

Men persevered and remained in the good graces of their wives and community. But they reached a point where they could no longer bear the tyranny. They hatched and slowly weaseled their way into a covert takeover. One by one, they impregnated their wives. While the women rulers wrestled with their hormones, morning sickness, and ballooning bodies, the men revolted. They overthrew the administration and replaced it with the patriarchal system that the Gĩkũyũ practice today.

(The legend does not explain how women lost their land ownership or inheritance rights, or whether the community had expected them to shoulder the same family responsibilities as men assumed after the coup.)

After the power grab, men restructured the system and outlawed polyandry. Instead, they introduced polygamy, which meant a man could marry multiple wives, provided he could afford to pay the bride price.

Society also expected a man to provide land and a stable homestead for his wife or wives and children. His social status diminished if he slackened or failed to meet his obligations; males in his riika or age group ostracized him.

Riika comprised young men and women who underwent circumcision rites of passage in the same season. Each riika had a formal name; this was one of the ways Agīkūyū marked their ages and historical milestones.

My father belonged to the 1913 Kīhiū Mwīrī age group that he shared with Jomo Kenyatta, the first president of Kenya. Men and women who belonged to the same riika shared a lifelong bond, similar to college fraternities or sororities. This meant that if, later in life, Baba had met Mr. Kenyatta and mentioned his riika, Mr. Kenyatta would have welcomed him and, at the very least, instructed his staff to treat Baba well.

Unlike today, when many men misbehave and feel little obligation to their communities, Gīkūyū tradition highly valued honor.

When a young man reached the age of marriage, he chose a young woman and then informed his father. The father and two friends paid a visit and introduced the matter to the young woman's parents. Or, the parents of the two young people arranged their marriage with their full knowledge. (Sometimes, a prominent family arranged for their young son to marry a young daughter from another prominent family once the two grew up, but such marriages were outliers.) This brought the two families together and cemented their friendship.

If a man itched to marry a second wife and had a prospect in mind, he consulted his first wife. This was not out of obligation but rather the norm for nurturing harmony in their homestead.

If he had not identified a candidate, his first wife helped him scout for a suitable one. She approved additional marriages unless she had fallen out of favor with her husband, in which case he married whomever he chose.

In most polygamous homes, the senior wife commanded respect and ruled over the co-wife or co-wives.

Sometimes, a polygamist wanted an additional wife, and his wives objected. When that happened, the senior wife threw vocal tantrums about the peril of a new wife coming to disturb the serenity in their homestead. Except for tyrannical men, most husbands conceded and abandoned the idea.

Polygamy also came in handy if a husband lost affection. He then married another woman and demoted his first wife to second-class status or sexually ignored her. No wife had this option, even if she no longer loved her husband. She stayed to raise her children.

When her son or sons matured and built their houses behind their father's homestead, one of them built a home for the mother.

∗

Gĩkũyũ men practiced (and a tiny minority still practice) polygamy for various reasons. First, the more wives a man had, the more children he brought forth, the more work they performed, the bigger the land he could own, and the more animals. A few men married tens of wives.

Polygamy was therefore a sign of wealth and prestige. Such men never did manual labor. They instead managed their animal herds and families. Display of wealth, then, just like today, nourished and massaged men's egos and garnered considerable power, besides a possible esteemed seat on the governing council.

A man's standing and level of involvement in the community depended on whether he had a wife or wives and children. No Gĩkũyũ man could play a role in governance without a family. Men dreaded ending up heirless; polygamy eased this fear by increasing the chances that a son would survive to carry on the lineage.

When daughters married, they joined their husbands' families, while sons remained as pillars of their families, clans, and community. If a man died without a son to take over as mũramati na mũtungatĩri (trustee and manager), his family's bloodline ended. To guard against this, parents bore as many children as they could, hoping enough sons would survive to ensure the family's continuity.

Polygamy also came in handy in cases of infertility.

If a first wife did not become pregnant for an extended period, she anguished. Meanwhile, her in-laws complained their son had married a thata (barren woman), while the community, especially the women, showered her with pity, implied or behind her back. Eventually, the husband married a second wife.

Most times, the infertile wife helped choose a young woman whom she believed would fit well into their prospective polygamous family.

When the co-wife bore children, the wives raised them together, and the children added an adjective after maitũ (mother) to differentiate between the two: maitũ mũkũrũ (senior mother) or a plain maitũ to refer to their birth mother. If their father married another wife, the children referred to her as maitũ mũnyinyi (junior mother).

Because there was no family without children, polygamy minimized or removed the stigma of infertility in cases of sterile women.

As for male infertility, if a first wife failed to conceive, a man married a second wife. If the new wife failed to get pregnant for an extended period as well, whispers about the man's fertility festered. However, this possibility and how to address it had already been addressed during the rites of passage when young men and women in their mid and late teens had learned about sexuality and adult responsibilities.

So when a husband became a "suspect," the younger wife stepped up to rescue his honor. She improvised and brought forth children through surrogacy.

If a wife took too long to act, her mother-in-law nudged her.

"There is no difference between my son and his agemates," she would say, implying it was about time the daughter-in-law chose a surrogate father among her husband's age-mates.

The man thus chosen obliged and shut his mouth to avoid embarrassing her husband.

Children born of this arrangement never learned that the man who raised them was not their biological father. The adoptive father may have suspected, especially if the children resembled the surrogate. But such a father kept his suspicions to himself, happy he had a family, and his infertility remained private. (Most times, the first wife joined the surrogacy and got her own brood. In surrogacy cases, however, families ended up with fewer children.)

The Gĩkũyũ community never considered wives bearing children with their husbands' agemates as infidelity, shameful, or dishonorable. It fulfilled a need, much like today's surrogacy or sperm donors.

The death of a spouse was another reason for polygamy. Unlike today, the Gĩkũyũ people did not practice single parenthood. A widower soon remarried and vice versa.

If a husband died, his widow would often marry her brother-in-law to keep the family together. If her late husband had no brothers, she married a widower, and the two merged their families, or someone married her as his second wife.

Polygamy also curbed men's infidelity, especially when their first wives reached menopause. Men itched to marry second wives, while first wives longed to "retire." The wives had no illusions about their sexual prowess and happily helped court suitable wife candidates for their husbands to consider and marry.

Since men remained tight-lipped about the reasons for their plural marriages, at least in mixed company, I never heard a single man discuss his purely selfish motive.

But it was an open secret that, despite the high value men placed on children, they found them bothersome until those children grew old enough to run errands, herd animals, or work the land. Sometimes, a man would marry a second wife to escape his first wife's demanding child-rearing.

When the second wife bore children, and the first wife's children were still dependent, the man might marry a third wife. By the time the third wife brought forth her own brood, the first wife's children would be grown. The man then weaseled back to his first wife and nurtured a closer liaison.

If a man could not afford bride prices for multiple wives, he confined himself to thingira, the man-cave sanctuary, which I suppose came about for that purpose, avoiding rackets of young children.

*

The Gĩkũyũ started phasing out polygamy after Britain invaded and occupied Kenya, which resulted in smaller landholdings. The colonial government also levied the so-called hut tax based on the number of houses in a homestead. This meant the more wives a man married, the more houses he owned, and the higher taxes he paid.

To operate in the new cash economy, men had to leave their families and communities and trek long distances in search of work. They found jobs on European farms and in towns, which made mobility and unstable living conditions another polygamy deterrent.

Today, although polygamous Gĩkũyũ families are uncommon, one can still spot an occasional husband with two wives.

And although women are against polygamy, a minority of them still support it. Some people claim these supporters are mistresses who want the law to help them emerge from the shadows. They may have a point because I doubt there is a single working-class Gĩkũyũ man with two wives. I've heard quips like, "I can't afford the one I have at home."

As of this writing, Muslim and customary (traditional) marriages are polygamous under Kenyan law. A man can marry multiple wives, provided he follows the established process and no person objects to his application for registration.

*

My father wrestled with polygamy for about twelve years, but never thrived in it. Otherwise, on both sides of my family, from my great-grandparents to this day, no one else has indulged in polygamous unions.

15. Child Purchase

Those beliefs about marriage, fertility, and lineage were not abstract ideas in my family; they shaped my father's earliest marriage in painful ways.

Baba and Kaguyu, his first wife, married at the end of World War I. They lived on the plot at Kahiga-inĩ in Nyeri that Baba, as a teenager, had carved out and cleared before the British zoned community lands.

He planned to establish a home and raise a family. But to his and Kaguyu's anguish, several years passed without her getting pregnant. Meanwhile, they learned of a famine in Meru, where they could buy a female child for a sack of maize; boys were not for sale.

When they decided to buy a child, Baba consulted travelers familiar with Meru. They told him of an old woman (whom I'll call Kendi) who accommodated lodgers. He sent word that he and his wife would arrive at her home within the month.

Baba and his bride, in the company of other travelers, trekked to Meru, about 50 miles away. He carried the sack of maize while Kaguyu carried the supplies they needed during their safari.

They plodded along a well-traveled footpath through a wilderness of trees and thick underbrush, home to elephants, leopards, buffalo, wild hogs, and other wildlife.

They rested at dusk and slept in turns next to bonfires they built from dead tree branches, not only to keep warm but also to ward off animals they heard growl and grunt at night.

With heavy loads, it took them a week to arrive at Kendi's house.

The following day, they accompanied someone to an intermediary's homestead. After exchanging pleasantries in the man's thingira, one man helped Baba carry the sack of maize from where he had left it in the courtyard. He scooped the required amount of maize, using the two-mug mũraũri (goblet) with a white interior and blue exterior that Baba had carried for that purpose.

The intermediary sent for the biological parents to bring their young daughter so Baba and Kaguyu could see her.

The girl looked about four years old, which the prospective parents welcomed. They had already agreed to get the youngest child available, whom they planned to pamper until she forgot her parents and her previous life.

The girl's biological father told Baba and Kaguyu to fetch their new daughter the following morning.

When they returned, they found the so-called biological father and another man waiting for them in the intermediary's thingira. Kaguyu waited outside, seated on the granary's jutting boards.

"The girl is in nyũmba," the intermediary told Baba when he joined the men.

"Since we have settled the matter," Baba said, "can we have the child? My wife and I would like to leave tomorrow."

The biological father called out to his wife to bring the girl. When the woman entered, a scruffy, much older girl followed behind, biting her fingers, her head bent to one side.

"This is not the same child!" Baba said.

"What's the difference?" the intermediary asked. "A child is a child."

"What happened to the one you brought us yesterday?"

"She's not available anymore."

"My wife and I came all this way to deal with lying grown men?"

"Return to nyũmba," the intermediary told mother and child. "We'll call when we need you." He didn't want Warama airing his ire in their presence.

Baba finished his complaints by calling the men sneaky and dishonorable.

The men did not protest or explain their behavior.

"I have to discuss this with my wife," Baba said.

Outside, he and Kaguyu talked and made their decision.

"We want a young child," Baba said when he rejoined the group. "But I didn't bring my wife all this way to return empty-handed. We'll take the older girl."

"Things are not good," the intermediary said, shaking his head. "The girl's mother changed her mind. She has already left with the girl."

Baba and the child sellers exchanged heated words that, under different settings, would have resulted in a fistfight.

Crushed, he and Kaguyu left in disgust and humiliation.

*

On their second trip, Baba and Kaguyu were swindled again. After the transaction, the person sent to bring the girl claimed a relative had taken her away.

When they returned to Nyeri, on the verge of giving up, they failed to understand why the children's parents changed their minds or became sneaky and hostile at the last moment. Because they spoke only a little Kimeru, Baba and Kaguyu figured they could have misunderstood the amount of maize the parents required.

On their third and last trip, the couple carried a bigger sack of maize in case that was the problem.

Just like before, Kaguyu's load became lighter as they depleted their supplies. She was not very tired when they arrived at Kendi's house. But when Baba dropped his heavy sack, he felt so drained and fatigued that he could not sit upright. Kendi showed him a plank bed to stretch and rest. He slept for two days and awoke on the third day.

"When I awoke," he said decades later, "it was as if I had been in a coma."

The next day, Baba and Kaguyu visited the girl's parents. When he said they brought a sack of maize, the father balked. For his daughter, the man said, he wanted the sack to contain equal amounts of maize and njahī (white-eyed peas).

Baba became so stupefied that he could not verbalize his discontent. Defeated, he shook his head, turned, and walked away. Kaguyu clicked her tongue and followed her husband.

Back at Kendi's house, Baba sat and hung his head.

When Kendi learned why Baba looked so distraught, she showered him with blessings.

"Don't worry, Warama," she said. "Children will fill your home to the brim like this, Clap!" She clapped her hands to show how many and to seal her prediction.

To Baba, Kendi's words sounded hollow, like nonsense. He took her for a senile old crone and waved his hand toward her dismissively.

Undeterred, Kendi repeated her prediction.

"Come on," Baba said to Kaguyu. "Get ready. We'll leave early in the morning."

After supper that evening, Kaguyu talked sense into her husband. They rested for another two days before they joined another caravan of travelers headed back to Nyeri.

On their way home, Baba and Kaguyu lamented their fruitless endeavor—a total waste of time and energy, they said. Frustrated, Baba declared they would never try to "buy" a child again.

When they arrived, however, he performed a small act of reclamation: he took the goblet he had used to scoop the maize, declared it a family heirloom, and tucked it away in his trunk. As they grappled with the quiet of a childless home, Baba eased their burden by announcing they would become *athomi* (readers) like some of their neighbors. They had observed that nothing seemed to faze the *athomi*; for them, every hardship was simply the will of God.

But the goblet did not stay hidden forever. Years later, when Baba's daughters—the children they once thought they would never have—prepared to marry, the vessel reappeared. Once a suitor completed the final traditional rites, Baba would retrieve the goblet from his trunk and fill it with homemade beer. He would then ask the man to drink; even for a non-drinker, a single sip was required. This shared drink was the final seal of belonging, signifying the man's formal acceptance into the Warama family as a true son and brother.

During that period, European missionaries campaigned fervently to convert the Gĩkũyũ people to Christianity. They referred to those who practiced Gĩkũyũ spirituality as plain Agĩkũyũ and those who converted to Christianity as Athomi, "readers," people who read the Bible.

Kaguyu started attending church sporadically. But Baba took longer to come around. But he stopped frowning and making mean comments about the foreign religion.

By the year's end, as if infertility was not enough burden, Kaguyu suffered from a disease that they could not name or cure. Sometimes she became so sick that she had to stay home. Her stomach bloated all the time.

Helpless, Baba kept mum about the misfortune that weighed on him. No baby and now a sick wife? It could be a woman's issue, he consoled himself, caused by too many thoughts about a baby.

When Kaguyu continued to complain, they blamed it on her food sensitivity. But after she avoided the foods she suspected and even drank herbal soups to cleanse her stomach, the sickness persisted.

Finally, Kaguyu consulted the village's wise women before visiting a medicine man.

While the women tossed their ideas around, one woman suggested she give Kaguyu a massage.

In a minute, the masseuse burst out laughing.

"Don't tell me you didn't suspect," the woman said after her laughter played out.

"Suspect what?"

"You are suffering from pregnancy."

"Are you sure?" Kaguyu whispered.

"Of course, I'm sure," the woman replied. "You know how many children I have brought forth?"

Kaguyu could not return home fast enough to tell her husband.

Lo and behold! In four months, the couple welcomed their first baby girl, Wanjirũ-big, named after Baba's mother. They trailed off their Athomi path before Baba made time to attend church.

Meanwhile, Kaguyu had become so accustomed to her childless state that she once forgot her infant daughter in the garden and only realized it after she arrived home.

In the next two years, the happy couple welcomed a boy, Njerũ-big, named after Baba's father, and then another, Waigwa, named after Kaguyu's father. They became overjoyed at their good fortune.

*

Over the years, Baba reminisced about the quest and marveled at Kendi's prediction. But he never mentioned how long he and Kaguyu tried to "buy" a child. But the period spanned between four and seven years, depending on who told the story.

When I interviewed my mother for a college paper, she told me the couple had remained childless for six years. Even that isn't likely because the years don't add up; their first daughter, Wanjirũ-big, had mentioned she was born in 1923.

Finally, Gathoni, her sister, told me in June 2016 that, besides going to Meru, Baba and Kaguyu (her mother) had gone to solicit for a child near Lake Baringo, an area populated by Kalenjin people.

However, I never heard that story when my parents were alive, and I couldn't find another relative—all younger than Gathoni—to confirm it.

16. Bonus Son

While infertility and family concerns distracted Warama and Kaguyu, social upheaval and colonial culture that had begun before the turn of the century continued to press on.

When the British turned Kenya into a protectorate in 1895 and soon made it their home away from home, among other measures, they introduced a cash economy—a replica of the English system—to replace the native currency and barter system.

By the time they got everything in place and upgraded the protectorate into a colony in 1920, the colonial government now required each man to pay taxes in British shillings and pounds, known as the "hut tax," based on the number of houses on his homestead.

Before then, men worked on their land, took care of their families, livestock, and community, and traded with neighboring micro-nations.

The monumental change weighed heavily on adults, especially family heads. They had no choice but to change their lifestyles, work for their colonizers, earn shillings to pay taxes, and function in the new economy.

The job of tax collectors became increasingly complex, straining relations with the community as the collectors attempted to collect taxes or apprehend those who could not afford to pay. Sometimes the government confiscated livestock in place of money. When men resisted, the taxman and his assistants turned to threats or physical violence.

The new cash economy and taxation forced able-bodied men to abandon their families and flee in search of work in towns or on British-owned farms.

They returned home every few months or once a year to visit and take money back to their families.

The practice of fathers living away from their families persisted until the 1970s. By then, however, they returned at the end of each month after payday.

The separation of husbands from their wives and children—alien to the Gĩkũyũ—created absentee fathers. Men became alienated from family relationships and their communities, leading many of them, especially in towns, to engage in undesirable activities that led to transmission of diseases. It also turned many wives into heads of households.

Baba suffered the same fate.

Orphaned as a teenager, the oldest of four children, he and his family owned little that government officials could seize instead of taxes. In the ensuing argument, one tax enforcer struck Baba with a baton, a blow to his hip he recalled into old age, claiming, "This leg will be the death of me."

The altercation became Baba's breaking point.

In the mid-1920s, he could no longer bear living in Nyeri, his homeland. He left his wife, Kaguyu, and three young children and joined a migrant workers' caravan headed west toward the Great Rift Valley. He and his colleagues trudged through virgin land on footpaths, going from farm to farm in search of work.

Baba eventually found work in Solai, Nakuru County, on a farm managed by a British man the workers called "Kamunge"—a nickname adopted because his actual name was unknown or unpronounceable. Upon arriving, Baba moved into the workers' camp, a place people would later call *gwa-Gathũmbĩ* (Gathũmbĩ's). While most men, including Baba, eventually moved on to establish their own homesteads elsewhere, Baba being at Kĩrĩma-inĩ, his friend Gathũmbĩ made the camp his permanent home, and his name became synonymous with the land itself.

I don't know how long it took Baba to stabilize and return to Nyeri to fetch his family. But when he returned, he found what he hadn't bargained for. He found four children instead of the three he had left. How he reacted remains buried with the departed. But he and his wife settled the matter. He accepted the boy, a bonus son whom Kaguyu had named Werũ after her brother.

Meanwhile, Baba stayed, winding down his affairs in Nyeri, long enough to stray. He would later learn that the woman he had partnered with in Ragati Location had given birth to a baby boy, whom she named Mwangi (after Baba).

Decades later, my brother Ndurumo met that half-brother, then a middle-aged man. According to Ndurumo, he resembled Baba. He, Ndurumo, also said he had heard rumors that Baba would have married the woman as a second wife, but she did not seem like a suitable candidate.

Given Baba's situation, I doubt he could have afforded to marry her. Whatever the case, he bundled his family and turned his back on Gĩkũyũland.

His infidelity, unlike Kaguyu's, and the son who resulted from it, remained a blip, nothing worthy of mention in the family. I learned about the incident while researching material for this book.

However, Baba's long absence and their infidelities triggered quakes between him and his wife, which clouded their marriage for the rest of its duration.

*

According to family stories, Kaguyu could not settle at Kamunge's farm. No one seemed to understand her situation. She was a young mother with young children, stuck away in a rural enclave. To unsettle her even more, she gave birth to a baby boy—Mwai—who died in infancy.

In time, though, she and Baba ended up with five sons—Njerũ, Waigwa, Werũ, Mwai, and Gĩthũi; and three daughters—Wanjirũ, Gathoni, and Wairimũ. (Except for Mwai, the others lived well into their 80s and 90s, and the remaining two seem to enjoy their mid-90s.)

Despite producing more children than they expected, the marriage never thrived again. Over the years, the husband and wife became opposites. They disagreed about almost everything. For example, if Kaguyu said she would wait to tend her crops after the rain stopped, Baba would claim those were only droplets—an excuse for sloths to avoid work and stay home.

Tired of their wobbly marriage, Baba escaped into another woman's arms.

17. Nyachuru

Nyachuru's story, like many women's stories before hers, was shaped long before she was born.

Before foreign occupation fragmented the Gĩkũyũ nation, young men and women who underwent rites of passage became members of a nationwide riika (age group) with a formal name. Members of both sexes sang, danced, and socialized. Willing partners practiced safe sex known as ngwĩko, a non-penetrative practice.

A man gyrated his hips and rubbed his member on his partner's oiled thighs until he ejaculated. Tradition forbade men from tampering with the chastity belts young women wore. Occasionally, a young man lost control and forced his way in. Or a young woman got carried away and joined in her mate's enthusiasm. Blame always fell on the man, as society deemed women feeble-minded.

If the woman accused her partner of crossing the line of decency, the young man suffered the consequences when his age-mates and community ostracized him.

If the young woman became pregnant, the partners married. Sometimes the man denied responsibility, forcing the woman into a trial. But no woman became pregnant and refused to marry the responsible party. Otherwise, her father married her off as a second wife. Unlike today, society did not tolerate single motherhood.

In the early twentieth century, ngwĩko practice died out because of migration to farms or towns, or to war, where people lived among communities of different cultures.

Even in homogeneous communities such as Nyeri, customs and traditional safeguards lost their potency, replaced by new colonial laws that did not address the natives' basic concerns. Wrongdoers did not have to remain beholden to their communities. They left and got work elsewhere among unknown, diverse people.

Those were the circumstances in Tũmũtũmũ, Nyeri, under which Nyandia, the woman who would later become my maternal grandmother, gave birth to her Oops child in or about 1910.

Most likely, a young man forced himself onto Nyandia and disappeared when he learned of the outcome. Except for the child, the incident remained a family secret. The few members of Nyandia's family who knew what happened are all long dead.

Bearing a child out of wedlock brought Nyandia's family enormous embarrassment. They sealed their lips and pretended nothing out of the ordinary had happened. Nyandia gave birth and named her little Oops Nyokabi after her mother.

Baby Nyokabi grew into a healthy, energetic toddler. Her grandmother and other women claimed the little girl rushed churu, churu, churu, churu (here, there, here, there). In time, the women coined the name Nyachuru, a busybody who does the churu.

Was this incidental? Did the women know the name Nyachuru had another meaning? I'd learn about this years later.

However, in time, the name Nyokabi faded into the background.

"Nyokabi" means from ũkabi, or Maasai. The adoptive family gave my great-great-grandmother the name after warriors captured her from the Maasai nation as war booty following the Gĩkũyũ and Maasai livestock raid. (The Gĩkũyũ did not harm females during warfare; captured girls were absorbed into the tribe.)

The Maasai may have practiced the same. My brother, Ndurumo, told me about an elderly Maasai woman he met while working in Narok in the late 1970s. When his workmate took him to visit their Maasai boma (homestead), Ndurumo met the old woman basking in the sun, leaning back on a wall. Besides nodding when his colleague introduced his grandmother, Ndurumo could not talk to her because she spoke no Kiswahili.

Halfway through his visit, he wandered the yard, fascinated; it was his first visit to a *boma*. The woman beckoned him.

"Umĩte mwena ũrĩkũ wa Gĩkũyũ?" (Which area of Gĩkũyũland are you from?) the woman asked, haltingly. But she remembered enough to know he was a Kikuyu.

Surprised, Ndurumo hesitated. "I'm from Nakuru," he said. "How did you learn to speak Gĩkũyũ?"

The old woman chuckled. "I became a Maasai as a young girl," she said. "But I have forgotten most of the language. Were your parents born in Nakuru?"

"No," Ndurumo said. "They came from Nyeri."

"What are their names?"

"Warama and Nyachuru."

"Did you say Nyachuru?"

"Yes, that's my mother's name," Ndurumo said. "But it's a nickname."

The woman chuckled before telling him that, among the Maasai, *Nyachuru* refers to a woman who was married during a light drizzle. If such a woman gives birth to a daughter, she names her Nyachuru.

Because my mother was named after her maternal grandmother Nyokabi aka Nyachuru, this means her great-grandmother—whose name I do not know—may have been the one the Maasai took. Some abducted girls resigned themselves to their new lives and were fully assimilated into the Maasai community. Others never did.

According to family lore, this woman did not give up. Through information passed quietly by traders, her people learned where she was. She was eventually rescued or found a chance to slip away and returned to Gĩkũyũland as a grown woman.

How she came to name her daughter Nyokabi after returning remains unclear. Perhaps the name lingered from a life she could not entirely shed. Perhaps it was memory, habit, or a mark of survival. What is certain is that she never settled in one place. She moved from Nanyuki to Naru Moro, then to Kĩa-Njogu, Thĩgĩngĩ, and finally Tũmũtũmũ—as if motion itself had become her inheritance.

*

As it occasionally happened, if a young woman became pregnant out of wedlock and did not marry the responsible party (who may have paid a fine or taken off), she married an older married man or a widower. Nyandia beat the odds when she married Ndurumo, son of Kĩbachwa and Kagendo. When her daughter, Nyokabi, also known as Nyachuru, reached the age when she could tell who was who in her household, Ndurumo was the father she found.

Nyandia suffered several miscarriages. However, in 1923, she gave birth to Nyachuru's brother, my uncle Eliud "Njoroge" Machira Ndurumo (1923 - 5/22/2022), whom my brother Machira is named after.

When Uncle Machira reached three or four years old, his family left Nyeri in search of a better life in the Rift Valley. On the way, they passed through a colonial farm in Nanyuki where Nyandia's brother and his wife lived. They left their children with their uncle, planning to fetch them later, once they had jobs and stabilized.

Ndurumo and Nyandia found work at Major Holman's (Horoma's) farm, east of Kamunge's farm. After they stabilized, they returned to Nanyuki and picked up little Machira, but left Nyachuru. She may not have known why her parents left her behind, since they never mentioned it.

Later in her mid-teens, Nyachuru left her uncle's residence and joined her family at Horoma's. My uncle was too young to know who decided his sister should rejoin the family. Based on Ndurumo's later behavior, however, he may have chosen.

If he left Nyachuru to become of age at her uncle's, it was likely her uncle would receive the bride price when she married. I doubt Ndurumo wanted to take that chance. Except for his one young son, who would expect help with the bride price when his time came to marry, Ndurumo had no other daughters. He therefore needed to have Nyachuru under his roof.

As Nyachuru matured, she fetched water, cut and hauled firewood on her back, gardened, and helped in other household chores. She also picked pyrethrum at Horoma's and coffee cherries at the neighboring farms to the west. It so happened that one farm where she picked coffee cherries was Kamunge's, where Baba worked as an overseer.

Baba noticed Nyachuru's work ethic from afar. This coincided with his search for a good wife candidate to insulate himself from his turbulent first marriage. After he observed Nyachuru for a while, learned her identity, and assessed her character, the chase was on.

Nyachuru could not stand Baba's advances; he was much older than she was, and the worst part was that she learned he was married.

From a young age, Nyachuru had observed a polygamous family next door where the senior wife ruled over her much younger junior co-wife as if the senior wife were the mother or the husband. She also heard women talk about authoritarian senior co-wives. When she came of age, she promised herself she would never become a co-wife.

But Baba would not quit. Whenever he tried to talk to her, however, Nyachuru would snicker or ignore him altogether.

One day, while walking through the savanna, she saw a man in the distance. When he reached closer, and she recognized Baba, she rushed several yards inland to avoid walking near him. When he reached parallel to where she stood, he wiggled his index finger at her and said, "Ndurumo's daughter, one day you'll become my wife."

She muffled a laugh.

"You'll see."

She returned to the footpath after he walked a distance away.

*

Baba was no catch. He was about twenty years older than Nya-churu—an older, married man—the exact type she had sworn never to marry. No man in her family had married more than one wife.

But Baba kept at it, waiting for Nyachuru to come around. If she remained stubborn, he, Warama son of Njerũ, would find a way to marry her.

She remained stubborn. With no other option, Baba side-stepped her and sent a message to Ndurumo that he, Warama, wanted to "visit" the family, a code word meaning he wanted to ask for Nyachuru's hand in marriage.

On the agreed date, Baba and his entourage of three men traveled to Ndurumo's homestead. Warama's hopes rose when they arrived. Ndurumo owned a small homestead that con-tained three houses—thingira, nyũmba, a granary, and a small goats' cottage—a man who could give in to persuasion to in-crease his herd.

After Ndurumo and his two friends welcomed the visitors, the group sat in his thingira, where women who helped Mrs. Ndurumo cook served them. When the men finished eating and the women cleared the dishes, Warama's representative opened the formal proceedings.

"My colleagues and I came to introduce ourselves," the man said, "and to ask you to allow the daughter of this homestead to join Warama's homestead."

"We welcome you to this homestead," Ndurumo said.

After pleasant, noncommittal exchanges, as was customary, Ndurumo needed to consult his daughter before starting the formal proceedings.

"Machira," he called out to his young son. "Go tell your sister to come."

Nyachuru entered thingira and stood by the doorway.

Ndurumo pointed at one man. "This man's name is Warama," he said. "Do you know him?"

"Yes," Nyachuru said.

"He came to this homestead because of you," Ndurumo said. "Before I discuss anything with him, I want to get your confirmation. Do you want to marry him?"

"No," she said hastily. "He has another wife."

Ndurumo squinted at Nyachuru and paused, perhaps unintentionally. It made it clear to the guests that it was not the answer he expected. Then he said, "You can go now."

That'll show him—coming here while he knows I don't want him, Nyachuru told herself. She could not return to nyūmba fast enough to tell her mother how she had embarrassed Warama in front of the men.

She had become appalled by his audacity when he sent a message that he intended to visit, but more so when they followed through.

"That man has no shame," Nyachuru said. "I've told him over and over that I don't want to marry him. What did he expect?"

"What did your father say?" her mother asked.

"Nothing."

"Nothing at all?"

"What could he say? I don't want to marry a married man."

*

Nyachuru's sunny and industrious disposition worked against her. The old and the young admired her. Men preferred her type—fertile, outgoing women who did not flinch at hard work.

But the young admirers she hoped to marry did not own goats or money. Without well-to-do fathers to help them with the bride price, they promised to pay it in installments.

Unfortunately for her, Warama, son of Njerũ, was ready, able, and eager to shell out the full bride price. It depressed Ndurumo to think he could pass up such an opportunity. About three years prior, he had listened to one of those bride-price installment young men. Things did not end up well.

Why should I miss a chance to boost my meager herd? Ndurumo must have asked himself. I would also get a lump sum of shillings, an amount I have never managed to save.

Ndurumo was no workaholic. He watched over people who picked pyrethrum or did other farm chores. The man shunned manual labor as if it were an infectious disease. He never even helped his wife to cultivate the piece of land where his family grew food.

As the first son of Kĩbachwa, and the looker in the family, Ndurumo towered over his brothers, who were at least five-feet-ten-inches themselves. He displayed symmetrical features and soft hands with long manicured nails, a relic of a Gĩkũyũ elder.

Like many men of that era, Ndurumo managed his homestead with a firm, tyrannical hand. Nyachuru's rejection did not slow him. He had entertained his future son-in-law and his friends as if Nyachuru had said "yes" to the marriage proposal.

After the men left, Ndurumo talked to his wife.

"You'd better talk to your daughter," he told her. "Those men didn't come all that distance to visit this homestead to waste their time."

"What did she say?" Nyandia asked.

"I said to talk to her."

Nyandia was caught between her husband and her daughter. Like many wives of that era, she knew her husband's word was final. She did not dare attempt to change his mind.

Her out-of-wedlock pregnancy, miscarriages, and deaths of multiple children, besides her husband's narcissism, weakened her position in the marriage. Sometimes, Ndurumo implied she was lucky he had married her.

Despite Ndurumo's heavy-handedness, Nyachuru remained steadfast; she did not want to marry Warama, and that was that.

18. It's a Man's World

Nyachuru thought highly of herself. As a young woman, she had vowed never to marry a polygamist. With her outgoing disposition, she believed only lesser women agreed to be co-wives and live under the shadow of senior wives.

She planned to marry a man her own age, like her mother, a man who cherished monogamy. If her husband later married a second wife, she figured, at least she would occupy the respected first wife's slot.

Nyachuru was ahead of her time in thinking her ideals mattered to Ndurumo. She soon learned her standards could not withstand a man's world.

Ndurumo, son of Kĩbachwa, scoffed at what he called wendo foolishness. To him, love would develop after marriage. If it failed, oh well, Nyachuru would still have an established husband to provide for her and her future children. And he, Ndurumo, would have the bride price—goats and a wad of shillings—to show for it.

But Nyachuru overlooked those benefits and remained adamant in her resolve.

Meanwhile, Warama was eager to begin marriage negotiations. Whenever he and his entourage sent a message requesting a second visit, Ndurumo claimed he was not ready to receive them. The excuses made him appear a man with no control over his own homestead.

Embarrassed and troubled by how he seemed to his potential son-in-law, Ndurumo vowed to nudge his daughter to change her mind.

But how would he do that? Short of beating her, what else could he do? In Gĩkũyũ tradition, however, he could not touch her; a daughter's discipline fell on her mother. Ndurumo could do nothing except give up or turn on his wife.

"Did you talk to your daughter?" he started, followed by verbal abuse, accusing his wife of failing in her duties.

When that failed, Ndurumo turned to physical violence. Not a week passed without a verbal zinger or physical violence toward his wife.

The violence at home tortured Nyachuru. She felt cornered and cried for her mother. Yet, her mother endured the poor treatment and never once pressured her daughter to change her mind. The guilt agonized Nyachuru even more.

"I felt as much pain as if he were beating me," she later said.

In time, Nyachuru came to feel responsible for her mother's suffering. No one else could stop it but her.

Her resolve faltered, and she accepted the marriage proposal.

She and Baba married in early 1937.

*

Within the year, Baba took Nyachuru to meet his sister, Julia, who was then working as a nurse in Nairobi. He invited his oldest daughter, Wanjirũ-big, so she could keep Nyachuru company when his sister took him to visit her workplace or other places they could not go as a group.

Baba likely intended to console his new bride and to prove he was a better provider than any of those poor, snotty young men she wanted to marry.

For their first major outing, Aunt Julia arranged with a doctor she worked for to get tickets to the Nairobi Ngong Racecourse, about three miles from the city center. Although Aunt Julia had told them about the special tickets and what to expect, they didn't fully understand until they arrived.

Despite having *special* tickets, the gatekeepers told them to wait by the gate. White patrons gawked and frowned as they passed by the African guests. But a handful of them needed a more potent act to register their disapproval than mere frowns. They zigzagged off the walkway toward the guests.

"Get out of the way," they said.

Aunt Julia and her guests waited until all the privileged entered.

Again, they approached the gate where two men had just finished taking tickets.

"You can't get in here," one man said.

But the good doctor already understood how childish and low his tribe could stoop to thwart anything that would benefit the natives. He had gone before the official opening, talked to one gatekeeper, and signed his guests in.

During the back-and-forth exchange, one gatekeeper remembered the sign-in and allowed Aunt Julia and company to enter.

As they entered, Baba, in sandals, knee-high shorts, a shirt, a coat, and a hat, and Aunt Julia in a dress and shoes, and both used to dealing with white men, held their own. But Nyachuru and Wanjiru-big in traditional cloths tied over shoulders over skirts and shoeless, and having never seen more than two white people in one place, let alone a whole racecourse—behaved like timid rural children. They looked around, frazzled and conspicuous in an all-white-only domain. Africans entered there only to clean the stables, to tend to the horses, or to serve.

Meanwhile, the privileged stared, wearing surprised frowns. Some turned side to side, alarmed, as if a predator had appeared in their midst, and they expected someone to save them from the imminent danger.

The need to install segregation signs at the racecourse besides the "colored" bathroom for the workers had never arisen; natives were interested in their lost lands and equal and human rights, not going to a racecourse to watch horses outrun each other.

But with the four "intruders," everyone expected the colonial culture to settle matters without fuss. None of them expected the four Africans to proceed to the empty seats in the stands. And if they dared take the seats, the police would get involved because something bad or harmful would happen to those chairs, although none of the protesters could guess what.

After Aunt Julia's party endured the stares long enough, they proceeded to a grassy area between the stands and watched the races from there, sitting or standing.

The only satisfaction my parents took from the racecourse was that they went where others could not and watched white people, all stiff in white or khaki clothes and hats, involved in a mundane activity. Otherwise, watching horses gallop was a waste of their time, Mother said, the one time I heard her mention the horses.

But they enjoyed one place—at least my mother did—when Aunt Julia took them to watch a dance at Kaloleni Hall, east of the city center.

Years later, Mother said she had never seen such an impressive place. Music flowed from an accordion and karing'aring'a, a metal ring, while well-dressed people with polished black shoes slid around on the floor.

Hands in a prayer stance, she slid her palms up-and-down, up-and-down, while she mouthed shhh—shhh—shhh, the smooth gliding sound the dancers' shoes made. At such a climax, Mother said, she never heard a single peep—only music and shoes massaging the cement floor.

She enjoyed mwomboko dance the most.

In mwomboko, dancers take long steps similar to those in a tango. At intervals, the men gyrate their partners' waists and lift them straight up, inches off the ground, as if weightless, sometimes as high as a foot or two. (Men don't raise their partners while they dance on concrete—perhaps a couple of inches or so).

The Nairobi trip never lost its charm right up to Mother's waning years.

*

When my mother married Baba, he assigned Gathoni, his seven-year-old daughter, to Mother as a companion and "messenger," since Mother had no children. They called each other *Wathurutia.*

Despite the warm welcome into Warama's homestead and the excitement of the Nairobi trip, Mother soon learned that her fears about marrying a man with another family were well-founded. Kaguyu and Baba lived combative lives. Whenever they fought, Kaguyu disappeared for days or weeks, and Mother had to step in and care for her young stepchildren.

Although Mother never spoke of this to us, Gathoni later said she helped babysit Njerũ when he was an infant, though she was still too young to carry him in a ngoi. By the time Ndurumo was born, she was old enough to carry him on her back in a skin ngoi.

Nevertheless, Mother never softened her negative attitude toward polygamy. Even in my twenties, she warned me not only against polygamy but also against men with prior families.

19. Wife Runaways

Resistance for a wife took only one socially acceptable form: she ran to her parents when dissatisfied with her husband's conduct or tyranny, hoping the shame and burden of managing a household would prompt him to change his ways.

Most times when she arrived at her parents' homestead and aired her complaints, instead of sympathy, her father asked her, "Does your husband provide well for you and your children?" The answer was usually "Yes," which earned her little understanding, especially from her father, who most likely indulged in the same tyrannical behavior his daughter complained about.

My mother, believing her case needed intervention or a hiatus, expected to garner sympathy when she took off after six years of marriage, already with two sons, Njerũ and Ndurumo. She fumed, slung nearly three-year-old Ndurumo on her back, secured him with a cloth, and ran to her parents at Horoma's, two farms away. She left her five-year-old Njerũ at the mercy of Baba and his first family.

When Mother arrived at her parents' homestead, her mother sympathized, but what could she do? Her father said, "Rest for a while," implying Warama would see the error of his ways. But little Ndurumo, named after his grandfather, had no use for rest. He soon let his grandparents know he belonged to a different homestead. From the first day, he rushed to the entrance when his grandfather's now bigger herd piled in from the day's grazing.

"Baba's goats!" he said, running out to the courtyard to meet them. "Goats have come. Baba's goats come home."

In his small world, every goat belonged to his father.

By the third day, elder Ndurumo had had enough of the boy's utterances and, perhaps irked because what the boy said bore some truth. Many of those goats descended from the herd his father had paid for his mother's bride price.

"Return this boy home to his father," Ndurumo said.

Mother never ran away again.

In telling us the story, she omitted the reason she abandoned her marriage. We never asked her either. My parents rarely shared their personal stories with us. When they did, we enjoyed them so much we never thought to ask follow-up questions.

Whatever the case, most wife-runaways were symbolic protests, meant to punish husbands by showing them the home could not run as well or would collapse without their wives.

More often than not, the tactic worked. When a husband got bogged down by managing a household and could not bear another day without his wife, he suppressed his pride and fetched her.

But with a stubborn husband, too proud to concede, the wife enjoyed her break, got tired of waiting, swallowed her pride, and returned home.

On arrival, she skulked in case her husband was home, eased into her house, and started her usual chores. If the husband was home or when he returned, he pretended he never noticed her absence, and life went on.

*

Even in those days, my parents' marriage fell outside the norm. Parents did not force their daughters into marriage. But mothers nudged their daughters if they took too long to get mates. "How come you don't join your friends where they go?" a mother would ask, or "I hear so and so's daughter got married. Do you know she's younger than you?"

And fathers nudged their sons.

The only time parents pressured daughters or sons to marry was in cases of out-of-wedlock pregnancies. Otherwise, young men and women chose their mates, or their parents arranged marriages with the couples' full knowledge and agreement. Even in arranged marriages, the couple could opt out.

*

Later, after we moved to the village, when my siblings and I were still little, Mother cooked in thingira to save on firewood. She sat on one side of the fire, Baba on the other, while we flocked on the third side. On rare occasions, Baba came home drunk and took his spot. If Mother said something complimentary to him, he would quip, "I know I married a good wife," and leave it at that.

At one time, to our utter pleasure, he dived into an incident of their so-called courtship to prove it.

Mother countered it with the word, "Coercion."

Baba expressed the love and respect he had felt for her and explained how he respected and followed the traditional process.

The two challenged each other in jest, our eyes glued to them.

"All I'm trying to say is I got myself a good wife," Baba finally said.

"Me?" Mother asked. "Then you have my father to thank."

"I said you'd be my wife, didn't I?" Remember? And threw her a sly look and a handful of knowing nods.

"Only because you colluded with my father."

"Tell me who got it right, eh?"

Mother snorted and threw him an amused side glance.

*

My mother exalted herself and kept her mouth zipped about issues that put her in a bad light. I doubt she knew someone had entrusted me with a *just-between*-us whisper about her.

The tidbit, a mere mention with no details, rarely surfaced. But when it did—on very rare occasions—it was almost incidental, limited to a handful of select family members. I doubt most of my siblings learned of the whisper. I learned of the details years after Mother passed away and never shared them with anyone until I wrote them in this book.

The story was that, before Baba came along, Mother had married Baiya, a young man who had promised to pay the bride price in installments. Ndurumo had cursed his bad luck that he might join his ancestors in the spirit world before he received half of his bride price.

The young couple bore a son, whom they named Gĩthĩnji, after Baiya's father. For reasons that remain unknown, when Gĩthĩnji turned a year old, Mother gathered him up and returned to her parents' home. Gĩthĩnji died of high fever just months after Baba and Mother married. He was about two-and-a-half years old.

Mother never breathed a word about having a baby before Njerũ or her first brief marriage before she died.

When writing this book, her brother Eliud Machira "Njoroge" Ndurumo (1920-May 22, 2022), then a young boy, clarified and confirmed the story and provided me with the names.

As for Kaguyu, even with a co-wife as a buffer, she and Baba failed to revive their withered union. After Mother and Baba married, Kaguyu left her young children in Nyachuru's care several times.

For the sake of the children, Kaguyu and Baba continued their yo-yo marriage for another ten years before it collapsed.

By then, two of their sons and one daughter had married and started their own families; the bonus son was in his twenties, the youngest son, Gĩthũi-big, had gone with Aunt Julia, and the two youngest daughters were already teenagers.

Kaguyu and Baba separated in 1947.

20. Nyambura

If the end of Baba's first marriage brought him relief, it turned out to be short-lived. As his second marriage thrived and the homestead got crowded, as he might have longed for in his younger days, the family rekindled his restlessness.

Mother had five children who vied for her attention with Baba. We, her brood, warmed ourselves by a campsite-like fireplace, close to the center pillar in Nyŭmba, where Mother cooked our food. Three sturdy stone blocks supported a sizable pot. But years of fire had gnawed at the blocks, leaving them smaller and misshapen. A stone could tip or wobble if a child stepped on it, making them lose their balance and fall into the fire.

At one point, Mother got two replacements from the farm's quarry, where two stonecutters blasted and chiseled well-shaped blocks of building stone. If they made mistakes, they welcomed women scavenging for the defective stones so the boss would not see them if he stopped by.

Above the fireplace, *itara* (a raised wood platform) rested on four posts about seven feet high. That was where Mother stored the firewood when it became difficult to keep it dry during the rainy season. Otherwise, she kept piles next to her house or under the eaves.

With Mother's unending chores, she hurried through evening meals. On the days she cooked red beans, which gave Baba indigestion, or if she thought he would frown on what she had cooked for the day, she would prepare a separate dish for him.

Between her job, gardening, and raising five children, she lacked the time to prepare palatable dishes for Baba, let alone serve them to him.

Having not eaten since midday, because we never ate snacks between meals, Mother did not wait for it to cool before dishing it out. She ladled the food onto white enamel plates or bowls for the youngest among us. Then one of my brothers took Baba his plate. (Mother didn't deliver food to him anymore.) Machira always rushed to volunteer. Before Mother thought better of it, she let him. On two occasions, in his hurry, he dropped Baba's plate. He still took it to him, with only half remaining.

"Return it to your mother," Baba would say.

That meant double duty for Mother as she hustled for another plate.

Meanwhile, we placed our steaming servings on the floor beside us (or later in our laps) while we sat on the floor or on low stools. I ate from a small bowl or soup-type plate before my sister, Nyandia, grew old enough to share a plate with me.

My brothers—Njerũ, Ndurumo, and Machira—ate from one plate. They gobbled their food as if in a competition, swishing it to cool it by taking air in between their teeth with intermittent hisses. Machira complained he could not keep up and urged his brothers to slow down. But they ignored his pleas.

He did not complain when Mother cooked mataha or mũkimo, which lasted two to three days.

For my sister, Nyandia, and any other small child, Mother stirred the food in a bowl and blew on each scoop before feeding it to her.

Baba could hear our chatter and noise. Maybe he felt lonely and envied us.

His thingira, at about 600 square feet, was smaller than Nyũmba. A wall running through its center divided it into a sitting area and a bedroom, with the entrance at its center. Baba warmed himself by a fire similar to ours, which Mother kindled in the mornings and my brothers in the evenings.

When we all settled down to eat, my brothers finished their food first, and then Machira rushed to Baba's thingira to keep him company. Baba pretended he had eaten enough and gave Machira the leftovers.

"If Machira weren't your son," Baba said to Mother once, "I would think you starve the boy."

My mother, like any parent, had her blind spots. I doubt it ever occurred to her to serve Machira on a separate plate, or that she cooked less than her family needed.

Baba must have reached a tipping point, tired of the noise and hungry mouths around him, and escaped back to plural marriage.

He married another cook, Nyambura, daughter of Kĩboi.

*

My first awareness of Nyambura came when I noticed a woman standing by thingira's porch. For a fleeting moment, the sight confused me. She had pale brown skin and seemed skinnier and taller than Mother. (In 2016, my brother Ndurumo told me I was then three years old.)

Along the way, I overheard someone say my father had married another wife. Because I could not grasp what a wife meant, I dismissed it as an adult oddity.

Nyambura cooked and lived in thingira because she had no children. But according to custom, each wife in a polygamous home still sent food to the husband. So, Mother continued to send a dish to Baba in the evenings. Her only reprieve was that she and my brothers no longer had to kindle Baba's fire, and she no longer had to provide his lunch or morning tea.

In typical polygamous homes, when the food got to thingira, a husband sampled each wife's dish. He then chose his favorite dish and offered the rest to his children. To keep the peace, he alternated the dishes he ate. But sometimes things got sticky when a husband preferred one wife's dishes. Whispers then swirled that so-and-so cooked unpalatable food.

I never heard which food Baba preferred—Nyambura's or Mother's (Kaguyu was out of the picture by then).

But Mother did not concern herself with Baba's preference. She believed no woman cooked Gĩkũyũ food as well as she did. Besides, if Baba frowned at her food, which he did not, he would give it to none other than her children.

After Nyambura joined the family, other adjustments followed.

With no way to track Nyambura's movements, the occasional chicken feasts my three brothers enjoyed in the woods ceased forthwith. And violence against them spiked in the name of discipline.

Nyambura reported them for minor infractions, such as claiming they had taken goats to pasture late or that they did not respond when she called. Based on her reports alone, Baba beat my brothers.

"Keep away from my children," Mother said when she could not stand it anymore. "If you don't, I'll pound you like maize kernels in a mortar, unless you strap yourself to your husband every time he leaves for work."

In old age, Mother liked to reminisce about such stories. Besides the boys' issue, she claimed, "Nyambura treated me with disdain, as if I had no way of getting back at her. Huh!"

I suspect she itched for an opportunity to have a showdown with Nyambura, an opportunity that couldn't come soon enough.

21. Juggling Two Wives

The Gĩkũyũ saying that *axes in one bag are bound to knock against each other* proved true as soon as Nyambura learned her way around Warama homestead.

She didn't wait for my brothers to call her *Maitũ Mũnyinyi*, or Junior Mother, before she treated them with a firm hand as if her status as stepmother gave her authority over them. Njerũ and Ndurumo avoided her or behaved so docilely in her presence that she never realized that, out of hatred, they never mentioned her name.

Meanwhile, Baba, the polygamist, managed his household without concern, oblivious to the hostile undercurrent that ailed his two wives. He even failed to stick to the tried-and-true "separate but equal" crafty control tool. He began taking both wives to occasional parties, likely to harmonize them away from children and other distractions, and perhaps to show off to his friends.

One Saturday, the three of them attended one of those parties at Gathũmbĩ's homestead, which was situated at the original work camp Kamunge had established for the farm's workers. Gathũmbĩ, one of the original farmworkers and a principled man, had the place named after him by his fellow workers.

The party went well, with an occasional envious glance from a monogamous man or two toward Baba's direction.

On their way home, Baba led through the savanna while his wives followed, chattering away about the party before the two trailed off to family matters.

As Mother claimed later, the amount of alcohol they had drunk had not impaired them, but it had loosened their tongues to tell each other things they would otherwise not have dared mention while sober.

Now, as they strolled behind their husband, their loosened tongues fussed about who did what to whom.

Halfway home, the argument escalated to personal insults and attacks.

Finally, to one-up Mother, Nyambura fired a verbal bazooka.

"You are too old to take care of your husband!" she charged. "That's why he married me!"

"Uh! You are a prostitute!" Mother shot back, her body rising to tiptoe and dropping down, poking her index finger toward Nyambura. "Probably you are the one who proposed!"

"I'm a wife, just like you!" Nyambura fired back, her body shaking. "My husband married me because he couldn't stand you anymore!"

"You're jealous of my children, you barren prostitute!"

That struck a chord. Nyambura rushed at Mother like an American football tackler.

Mother saw her coming, dug in deep, and set herself to receive the blow.

The two flailed their arms, scratched, grabbed, and hurled insults at each other. In the chaos, like a flash, Nyambura snatched Mother's left thumb, stuck it in her mouth, and her teeth dug in.

"Let go! Let go!" Mother said while she scratched Nyambura's face. Thanks to garden work, Mother's stunted nails and callused hands traumatized her face, but failed to leave decent scratches. For better results, Mother's fingers went for the eyes.

Nyambura shrieked and let go of the thumb.

"I'll teach you a lesson today!" Mother said. "You'll never attack another woman again!"

The melee continued.

In the tussle, they fell and rolled on the ground.

Baba heard the quarrel but ignored his bickering *two axes in one bag* and strutted on. He expected them to sort out their differences and catch up with him.

But when he heard a thud, he realized the fight had taken a dangerous turn.

He turned around.

He couldn't see them. The wiregrass and scrub had swallowed them.

He rushed back and stood about ten feet away, and gawked in disbelief.

His wives wrestled and clawed as if on a mission to kill each other. Focused on their fight, they paid him no attention.

Baba approached, perhaps expecting them to stop when they sensed his presence. He was disappointed. He then forced himself between them and pushed each wife away, aborting the fight. They both tried to get around him, determined to land one more scratch or fist.

"If you fight again," Baba said, "I'll teach both of you a lesson."

The word of the homestead's ruler demanded a truce. The wives moved apart, breathed hard, but restrained their hands.

Baba gazed at them for a few seconds before he turned and led them home. Not another word passed between the three of them.

They arrived at dusk. Baba and Nyambura headed to thingira while Mother hurried to nyûmba to tend to her children. Before she started, she made a mug of tea for Baba, which he never skipped even when drunk.

His wives' fight must have disturbed him through the night, leading him to decide to teach them a lesson, even though they stopped fighting when he separated and warned them.

"Your father has many issues," Mother said when she told us the story years later. "He surprised me when he called me."

She knew Baba so well that she expected trouble before she reached to thingira. After she joined him and Nyambura, he called my brother Ndurumo.

"Bring me my whip," he said.

To make the bullwhip supple, he stepped onto the porch and cracked it several times while the two wives stood waiting.

When he determined the whip was ready, he addressed them. "Because you two craved a fight," he said, "you should fight properly and get it out of your system."

"Nyachuru, lie down on your stomach," Baba said, then turned to Nyambura.

"Whip mũiriguo [your co-wife] five lashes," he said. "After you finish, lie down, and she'll do the same to you."

He handed the whip to Nyambura.

"I will not whip anybody," she said, shaking her head. She then hugged her chest, her lips pressed tight.

A year into her marriage, Nyambura remained ignorant of the type of man she had married, a man who never reconsidered decisions no matter how silly, cruel, or unfair.

"All right," Baba said to Nyambura. "Then lie down." He handed the whip to Mother.

She, still bitter that Baba had aborted the fight before she "taught Nyambura a lesson," gave Nyambura five lashes with all the energy she could muster. Nyambura twitched after every whip landed but made no other moves.

"Now, give the whip to mũiriguo," Baba said.

Mother waited for Nyambura to get off the floor and compose herself.

When she seemed ready, Mother extended the whip to her.

Nyambura shook her head, pouted, and crossed her arms again.

"Okay," Baba said, "lie down, both of you."

He whipped them five lashes each.

"I never want to hear you've assaulted each other again," he said before he dismissed them.

Subsequently, if Baba wanted company, he asked one of his wives to accompany him at a time.

Mother accompanied him one more time.

"Have you fed the children?" Baba asked her when they returned home.

"I have leftovers," she lied.

There and then, Mother decided she would never again join Baba at a drinking party. She also stopped drinking alcohol and never touched it again.

22. Fruits of Polygamy

Orphaned as a teenager, Baba had one mission: to grow up, establish a homestead despite the confines of the colony, and continue his family's bloodline. This mission became even more critical when Mwai, his only brother, died in his prime and childless in World War I.

Baba's remaining sibling, Aunt Julia, walked out of her marriage as a young woman when her husband married a second wife after she, Aunt Julia, failed to get pregnant.

The only sibling who bore four boys (two of them named Njerũ and Waigwa, after their mother's father and brother) was his sister, Aunt Wairimũ, buried right there at Kĩrĩma-inĩ. But those nephews belonged to a different bloodline, a bloodline Baba scarcely cared about.

His poor sister had married a witchcraft peddler named Ndoogo. When she fell terminally ill, with no daughter to nurse her, he hauled her from Ragati, Nyeri, to Kĩrĩma-inĩ and deposited her at Baba's doorstep. "I'm unable to take care of her," he said. He left a day later, saying he would return soon to check on her.

Baba engaged a medicine man and then another. But Aunt Wairimũ continued to waste away. Hush-hush whispers circulated that her husband had poisoned her.

She hardly ate anything. The only thing she tolerated was porridge. The family stored it in a gourd for her. She warned several times that no one should drink her porridge; it was hers alone.

One day, she became chatty, which gave the family hope that she might pull through. Before midday, she said she felt an urge to eat goat meat. She insisted her brother get her some. She and Aunt Julia were the only people who could make demands on Baba, address him as equals, or throw verbal tantrums.

As Baba and my half-brothers slaughtered a goat, Aunt Wairimũ fussed, claiming they were taking too long.

Meanwhile, Baba asked someone to get the grill going. As soon as they opened the stomach, he cut out the liver and put it on the grill so his sister could eat and hush while they dismembered the carcass and roasted the meat. When the liver was ready, he cut half of it into bite-sized pieces for his sister.

"It's about time I ate this meat," Aunt Wairimũ said when my half-sister took her the plate. She steadied herself, propped on her elbows, and sat on the plank bed where she spent her days and nights.

She put her first piece in her mouth and chewed several times. Just before she swallowed it, she gasped as if the piece resisted going down her throat. She fell back, her hands splayed, and she drew her last breath.

"There's something wrong with Auntie," the children cried out. Baba rushed in and pried the piece of liver from her mouth, straightened her legs, folded her arms, and closed her eyelids.

He, Njerũ-big, and Waigwa dug a grave and buried Aunt Wairimũ the same day.

Two days later, the family saw no need to waste the porridge in the gourd. Before Kaguyu served it to the children, the gourd cracked clean in two, and the porridge flowed out.

As for Mr. Ndoogo, aside from the family's sightings in Nyeri, no one in Solai heard from him again.

*

So far, despite the colonial upheaval, Baba had reached his goal; he had established a semblance of a Gĩkũyũ homestead even if it wasn't on his own land.

So, when his two wives clashed, it blindsided him. But when he went over the matter, he realized the tension that smoldered within his family had started not long after he married Nyambura. It puzzled him that his wives could not get along. One wife had children, the other did not; they lived in separate houses and shared no kitchen facilities, supposedly the cause of many women's conflicts. What was there to fight about?

I doubt Baba considered sharing a husband a factor.

But based on the action he took, he had reached a stage where he admitted he had failed in his quest to attain distinguished Gĩkũyũ elder status with many goats, wives, and children, all living in harmony.

Meanwhile, gossip, which must have reached him, swirled that Nyambura had become friends with Kaguyu, the divorced first wife, who now lived at Kabati in her son Werũ's house while he worked at Bahati.

According to family members, whenever Nyambura went to her small garden at Kabati, she visited Kaguyu. During those visits, Kaguyu acquainted Nyambura with the family dynamics and taught her how to ingratiate herself with Baba and become indispensable.

"You are the bride and the favorite wife," Kaguyu told Nyambura. "Nyachuru will have to bow to your wishes."

Other rumors claimed Nyambura was infertile, the reason Mother threw *thata* (barren woman) shot at her during their fight and turned her into a thumb chewer. But I doubt Baba cared about that—he had more than enough children. Or infertility could have been the reason he married Nyambura.

The rumors failed to rattle Mother. She, already a mother of three sons and two daughters, had become too entrenched in the family to feel threatened.

By the casual manner in which she later told the story, including the news about the co-wife, perhaps she even felt relieved to have Nyambura around, if only she could leave her sons alone.

With her hands full, she had little time to spare for fights. So Mother threw herself into her casual job at Kamunge's, her garden, and her children. She produced enough food to go around. Besides the food and tea she made for Baba, she "headed" her own household.

But Nyambura continued to send Njerũ and Ndurumo on errands, unconcerned whether Mother had assigned them other duties. Although this irritated her, it was not the main rub. What irked her the most was that Baba punished the boys when Nyambura reported their lapses.

To minimize accusations, my brothers stayed out of Nyambura's way whenever they could.

But two-year-old Nyandia toddled across the courtyard and entered thingira at will.

"Give the child something to eat," Baba said when Nyandia stopped by.

"There is nothing left," Nyambura would say. Or, "I'm busy right now; I'll cook shortly."

"You have nothing in this whole thingira for a child?"

Nyambura would keep quiet.

*

Because Baba never talked about his family, nobody could tell how long he had agonized about the dynamics of his polygamous lifestyle and the disharmony it had brought to his homestead.

Two years after Nyambura joined the family, he showed how much the tension bothered him. He invited his friend Paul and another man early one Sunday, something no one did unless it was very important.

Nyambura made tea for them.

The men engaged in small talk while sipping their tea. As soon as they emptied their mugs, Baba made his intentions known.

"Nyambura," he called out.

"Yes?"

"Go through this thingira and pack whatever belongs to you."

Everyone froze, wordless.

"Kamwana's father, is there a problem?" Nyambura asked when she composed herself.

(Njerū was named after Baba's father. Nyambura called him Kamwana, lad, as a sign of respect. Daughters and sons-in-law never called their parents-in-law by their names, even the children named after those in-laws.)

"There won't be any debate or discussion," Baba said. "I just want you to pack."

Nyambura froze again—for a long, long time.

Tension built up, but no one spoke.

She then started packing.

How much could she pack? Except for her clothes, she owned nothing else besides memories of the two years that she needed to process as she walked about.

When she finished, she deposited her wooden box and two small bundles by the threshold and waited for Baba's next order.

"Paul?" Baba said. "Take this woman and hand her over to her uncle, Mũturi. I won't discuss this matter again. I don't even want a refund of my bride price."

The two men exchanged glances, got on their feet, and left with Nyambura in tow.

*

My father's divorce from Nyambura went against tradition. He invited the two men to our home and never said, at least to the family, why he sent Nyambura away.

In Gĩkũyũ custom, if a husband could not bear to remain married to his wife, he would send men to return her to her parents. A negotiation ensued to determine whether the husband should receive a portion of the bride price or forfeit the entire amount.

The representatives first explained to the parents why their daughter's husband had divorced her. Reasons included:

- Infertility
- Refusal to render conjugal rights without reason
- Practicing witchcraft
- Becoming a habitual thief
- Willful desertion

- Persistent gross misconduct.

Besides the above reasons, a wife could have divorced her husband because of cruelty, ill-treatment, drunkenness, and impotence.

*

In 2014, I interviewed Gathoni, my then eighty-four-year-old half-sister, and asked her why Baba divorced Nyambura.

"When Nyambura drank," Gathoni said, "she became unruly like a drunken man."

"What do you mean?"

"One day, she drank and became unhinged," Gathoni said. "Baba and another man took and locked her in thingira's bedroom to calm her. But she climbed over the wall and fell into the sitting area."

"I remember that commotion," I said. "I saw two men pick her off the floor."

"But that wasn't the only reason—"

"There were others?" I asked, leaning in toward Gathoni, ready to hear a family secret.

"Your mother contributed to Nyambura's marriage breakup?"

"My mother?"

"Yes, she undermined Nyambura's relationship with Baba."

Oh, please. Let Mother rest in peace! I wished I could tell Gathoni.

I suspected she believed her mother's marriage also broke up because of my mother, but I kept that to myself.

I recall two incidents about Baba and Nyambura's marriage. The first one is a blurred awareness of her as she stood by thingira's porch, her hand clasped around the post. The second time was during the commotion when she fell over the wall. Then she disappeared.

Serenity returned to our homestead as if she had never existed.

Not a single memory of Nyambura remained in the next two years before Baba received orders for us to move from Kĩrĩma-inĩ.

23. Kĩbagio

Polygamy caused rancor in our family because of jealousy and clashing personalities. But after Nyambura's departure, the restored peace inside our homestead did not shield us from the colonial antics.

Most people's anxieties, from which they could not disentangle themselves, came from the way the colonial government and its agents controlled, marginalized, and treated them poorly in their own country.

Since his youth in Nyeri, Baba had suffered under those oppressive laws—the reason he moved away.

When the British suppressed native uprisings and occupied Kenya, they established it as a protectorate to protect explorers and missionaries before turning it into a colony in 1920. Among other laws, they enacted one that restricted what Africans could plant or raise. One stipulation made it unlawful for Africans to raise billy and nanny goats.

But the British farmers did not enforce that law, at least not in Solai. When they noticed the infraction, they warned their farmworkers but did not follow through. Long-term employees like Baba began working for British farmers when some of them owned little and struggled to pay wages, wages that were funded by the work Africans performed. Focused on establishing themselves, the farmers did not scrutinize what their employees did in their spare time, scattered across sprawling farms with no roads but footpaths and a handful of tractor trails.

At Kamunge's farm, answerable to one man, for years, Baba felt insulated from many colonial troubles. He and his family lived on a secluded homestead, tucked away in one corner of the farm, with a footpath as the only connection to the outside world.

But finally, the law reared its head, and one tentacle reached out. It wasn't because of taxation, this time, which Kamunge deducted from his wages with no accounting required, but because of Baba's impressive herd of goats, the central pillar of his homestead.

In Gĩkũyũ tradition, the land came first, followed by goats. Besides barter, the community used goats as currency to settle debts, pay fines and bride prices, accumulate wealth, and provide milk and meat for their families. It was a sign of respect—it still is—if a person visited and the host slaughtered a goat.

Under the live-and-let-live approach, employees raised prohibited animals without concern. They not only admired the elegant, sculptural horns but also claimed that, unlike sheep or other varieties of goats, billy and nanny goats:

- Were more intelligent and easier to herd
- Clothes and straps made from their skins were easier to treat, came out softer, and lasted longer
- Meat was tastier and leaner because the animals ate a variety of leaves
- Provided milk for their children.

Nanny and Billy goats also hardly went astray when their herders got distracted while they climbed trees, constructed toys, practiced target-shooting, terrorized birds with their slingshots, or scavenged for wild fruits. Sometimes a young herder lost the outlawed goats, worried senseless, only to find the herd safely home.

In contrast, regular goats and sheep grazed on grass or plants closer to the ground. This made their products not as highly prized. People considered them dumber than the outlawed billy and nanny goats.

If their herder slackened on his duty, the regular goats never found their way home; they huddled around a bush and settled themselves for the night.

To help locate the goats if they strayed, Baba put bells around the necks of a handful of those he considered more intelligent than the rest. These were usually females with kids or dominant males. The kids wore smaller bells so their mothers could easily locate them and avoid distractions from their leadership roles.

Goat mothers, like humans, insisted on locating their kids when they romped with others around bushes. No goat agreed to leave for home or lead without her kid beside her.

Baba also branded some goats, mainly the neutral-colored ones with no notable marks, for easier identification if mixed with other herds.

Even with bells, the regular goats and sheep still became confused when it rained, got separated from the leaders, and became lost. This resulted in a search party of men in heavy coats, supplied as their work ration by Kamunge, and boys in raggedy calico shirts.

The searchers walked through the woods half the night and usually found the goats huddled together unless, on a rare occasion, one bumped into a predator.

So, in Solai, Nakuru County, and perhaps across the White Highlands (European-only settlements), peasants preferred rearing the forbidden billy and nanny goats.

It came as a surprise when, in 1945, *Kĩbagio* (indiscriminate "sweeper"), a white inspector with a handful of armed white police and a group of their African subordinates, the work bees, descended on our homestead at 5:00 in the morning.

To awaken my family, they banged on doors as only the police could. The grown-ups opened their doors to flashlights aimed at their faces.

"Where do the other goats sleep?" The inspector asked. Baba owned so many goats that he could not fit them all indoors.

He pointed to the goats' cottage.

The inspector then told him and his family to stand aside. My parents and the older children gawked in horror at the chaos as the gang of officials rounded the goats as they bleated and kicked. They loaded them, stuck like maize combs, into a procession of monster lorries of that era, which did not need proper roads to get close to our homestead.

They left five (forbidden) goats with orders for Baba to phase them out in two weeks.

Hours later, my family learned that similar raids had taken place across the surrounding areas.

With homesteads scattered throughout the farms, however, the authorities could not round up all the animals and carry them away in one swoop. By the time Kĩbagio reached some homesteads, their owners had already learned of the raid and hidden most of their animals in the woods.

The raiders delivered thousands of goats to a field in Nakuru Town, where the colonial administration auctioned them to members of the British settlers' network.

According to my brother Ndurumo, Baba lost about 200 goats.

*

After the two-week grace period, owning a single billy or nanny goat became a hush-hush affair. But Baba still kept a handful of them mixed with the regular herd. He phased them out in the next few years after we moved to a fenced village, and it became harder to conceal them. Up to the age of ten, I recall Baba slaughtered three nanny goats before they all disappeared.

I can attest that the meat was lean, without the fat I disliked, and it was tastier than the meat from the regular goats Baba usually slaughtered.

Because the animals ate leaves, Mother rinsed and strained the contents of the large stomach (abomasum), which resembled half-chewed gobs of green salad. She ended up with a dark green, thick liquid, similar to a smoothie. She then mixed a measure of it with maize flour and cooked us green porridge that she claimed was medicinal.

Without sugar, the porridge tasted bland and smelled leafy, which my siblings and I hated, but we tolerated it as we did medicine. I waited for the porridge to cool, opened my mouth, rested the rim of the mug on my lip, shut my eyes, and gulped the porridge down, taking one break halfway.

Mother put the rest of the uncooked mixture into a gourd to ferment for future use.

24. Goat Pedigree

When Kĩbagio and his backup descended on Baba's homestead, and they identified who they were, he said nothing. He stepped aside as ordered, tightened his jaws, and watched along with his family as the intruders whisked away most of his wealth—his goats.

The raid's effects, however, did not get swept away with the goats. According to Mother, Baba never talked about the incident. Instead, he became listless and stayed indoors the entire weekend, and even kept it up the following week when he returned home from work.

I now wonder whether it ever occurred to him that he caused equal, if not more, anguish to his family because, as the colonialists jerked him, he in turn jerked his family or became outright violent, especially to my brothers.

I know Baba loved his children in his own way, but I'm not sure where he put them in the hierarchy of importance. Land was the highest, but without it, honor and goats ranked very high with my father. Anyone in the family who tarnished his honor or upset his goats expected a bad day—a terrible day indeed.

Each of my brothers and half-brothers had had bad days during their herding tenure. Usually, when herders were involved in various activities, goats grazed, cared for their young, socialized, and waited. But occasionally, the animals strayed, got disoriented, and got lost in the woods, or helped themselves to people's gardens. This accounted for most of my father's violence against my brothers.

Regarding incidents before my birth, or when I was too young to recall, I include only those accounts I confirmed with victims or eyewitnesses.

I started hearing about the beatings two years after we moved to the village. A year later, at nine, I witnessed how lethal my father could be to my brothers.

*

Despite the seizure of Baba's forbidden goats, he still hid two or three of them in an enclosure in Nyũmba. He also kept a handful of them mixed with the regular herd. This included a pedigree billy goat with massive horns that rivaled those of a buffalo.

Trouble hatched from a friendly gesture when Baba's friend, Mũkuhĩ, envied that billy goat so much that he wanted an offspring from its bloodline.

The two friends agreed for Mũkuhĩ to bring his nanny goat to live among Baba's herd until it bore a pedigree.

At the time, Njerũ was dealing with hunger and neglect in Nyeri. And Machira, at five, had not become a goat herder trainee to accompany Ndurumo to the grasslands. Contrary to tradition, Baba had given our fourteen-year-old half-sister,

Wairimũ-big, a boy's job. He partnered her with nine-year-old Ndurumo.

I had heard the story of Ndurumo and Wairimũ-Big's ordeal, but it was not until 2016, decades later, that I asked Ndurumo about it. He confirmed the story and retold it blow-by-blow.

From the first day at the pastures, he said, the farmed-in nanny goat acted jumpy and refused to join the herd. She lagged and kept to herself. Wairimũ-big and Ndurumo rounded and shooed her softly until she calmed down and inched closer to the herd. But other times, she skipped away, ears perked like a wild animal, and grazed alone.

After two days of pure trouble, the two herders agreed that one should mind the nanny goat until she acclimated.

"That Saturday," Ndurumo said, "we rounded the herd to return home."

"The goat got used to the herd?" I asked.

"Are you joking?"

"No."

"The goat behaved like a possessed animal," Ndurumo said. "When either of us rounded that animal, it inched closer to the others, then freaked out and scurried away.

"One time, it stopped about twenty-five feet from where we waited with the herd. It then faced us head-on, ears perked, eyes dilated and crazed. But each time I took a step toward that goat, it backed several steps. After three tries, the goat turned, galloped, and disappeared into the woods."

"How did you get it back?"

"We looked everywhere," Ndurumo said, "and gave up just before dusk. We headed home in case it got too dark. We feared the herd would get disoriented. On arrival, we reported the incident to Baba without delay."

Besides Mother and Nyambura—the two wives—and the very young, the entire family joined the search party. Baba and one of my half-brothers each carried a flashlight. The others carried sticks and followed the person with the flashlight until their eyes adapted.

When the searchers reached the spot where the goat disappeared, they fanned out. They combed the area for hours but found no telltale signs.

Early the next morning, Baba skipped his market day to resume the search with others.

About two hours later, one searcher came to a brushy area. Strewn about were bloody leftovers of skin and bones. "Hey! Hey! Come over!" he called out, waving his arm.

"It's as if bulls fought here last night!" one searcher said.

Because of the violence that had flattened the vegetation, no clear paw prints remained to identify the predator.

Baba dismissed the searchers but remained in the woods, perhaps still wondering how to explain the loss of the goat to his friend.

He returned home about half an hour later.

Within five minutes, he called out to Ndurumo and Wairimũ-big. As they rushed to thingira, fear gripped them; they knew what awaited them.

They found Baba at the entrance.

As soon as they entered, Baba closed the door. A pile of fresh sticks stood by the wall.

Ndurumo and Wairimũ-big started to shake.

Baba took a stick from the pile and swung it. He swung and swung and swung.

The two herders hollered and apologized.

"We'll never lose another goat again."

"Baba, have mercy on us."

They should have saved their pleas.

When the beating became monotonous or his right hand got tired, Baba diversified.

Using long leather straps, he bound each child's hands in front and legs at the ankles, leaving about a foot of rope on each side. He then took the two ends and wrapped them around the center pole. The two herders lay on their sides on the dirt floor, hogtied around the pole.

Baba got a fresh stick and started another round.

"He beat us on our backs, legs, and arms until it didn't hurt anymore," Ndurumo said.

I interviewed Wairimŭ-Big a week later. Her version mirrored Ndurumo's.

"Baba stopped beating a child only when he became exhausted," Wairimŭ-big said, "and couldn't spare extra energy. He hated Ndurumo and me and beat us the most."

Even after sixty years, Wairimŭ-big's voice choked, and she had to pause several times. She broke down after she said Baba hated her and Ndurumo the most. She could not continue.

Despite Baba's violent bent, my young age shielded me somewhat from the abuse my siblings and half-siblings suffered at his hands. So, except for the time he whipped me at age four for potty training, my memory of my family in Kĩrĩma-inĩ is full of contentment.

Later, in the village, my relief came because of my gender—
fathers left the discipline of daughters to their mothers. In our
household, my mother was not into excessive violence. Besides
a pinch here and a swat there, which I don't remember suffering, but my sister claims I did, if Mother needed to do it, she
struck quickly; she was incapable of holding anger for long.

And Baba could not recruit me as a temporary goat-herder,
the only reason that would have compelled him to cross the
gender line and assault me. By then, I already held a full-time
babysitting job.

25. Wacky Discipline

Goats were not the only reason my father raised his hand in anger. But while they caused about ninety percent of the violence in my family, the other ten percent came from childhood transgressions and crimes. The chicken theft fell under this category, but my brothers lucked out. Nyambura had breezed into our courtyard before Baba caught up with them.

The other childhood crimes occurred because we did not grow fruit trees. Like the billy and nanny goats, the colonial administration prohibited Africans from growing perennials or cash crops. The officials did not give their reasons.

But, from gossip that trickled down to the village we moved to, people understood that if they grew unlawful crops, especially cash crops, it would dilute the British farmers' monopoly on trade.

On the flip side, the crops would have provided better nutrition for African families and enabled them to earn extra income to send their children to school. Most parents could not afford school fees. And without land or retirement, the income would also have given Africans something to fall back on when they lost their jobs.

The colonizers, however, expected Africans to remain contented as dependents, confined to cramped native reserves with no claim to permanent homesteads. Missionaries—and the African converts they had trained and indoctrinated—repeatedly reminded them that this world was not their true home. Their real home, they were told, awaited them in heaven, where they would find opulence laid out and suffering and death would be no more. There was even a popular song that women sang as they worked—Thĩ-ĩno ti yakwa, nĩ kwĩhĩtũkĩra…, this world is not mine, I'm just passing through….

For those who quietly wondered why the British themselves did not wait for that heavenly abundance, the answer was that they were God's chosen people, while Africans were a cast-off lot as descendants of Ham. Meanwhile, permanence, self-determination, and freedom were all tied to ownership—an advantage the colonial government reserved only for British landowners, who were free to cultivate whatever they pleased.

Fruits fell into the perennial category.

To ensure no employee planted a perennial plant behind his back, every year before planting season, Kamunge sent his tractor driver to plow the plots he allocated to his married male permanent employees. (He did this after the tractor had plowed and planted his plantations; the reason Mother complained that her maize was not ready before she stole Kamunge's maize.)

So, on Kamunge's farm, like on other European farms, fruits grew in the wild or in his orchard.

Adults and little children ate no fruit, while older children scavenged for certain fruits and berries in the woods when they were up and about. Parents warned their children of severe beatings and jail terms (this had already happened) if they ventured close to Kamunge's orchard. But which parent could guarantee his or her child would not fall into temptation?

I doubt it crossed my parents' minds that my brothers could get tempted, or even that they knew an orchard existed.

But Njerũ, at thirteen, and Ndurumo, at eleven, knew of the orchard through other goatherders. And they fell into temptation.

When the two went to the pastures, they banded with other boys and walked east for at least four miles to Kamunge's two-acre orchard, set behind the colonial house. They approached the orchard from behind, sneaked in through the barbed wire, grabbed some oranges each, threw them over the fence, and clambered out. After they ate their fill, they hid the rest for the following day.

Late afternoon, they headed home with a well-fed herd of goats.

Baba joined them as they shooed and corralled the goats into their cottage. While Baba and Njerũ secured the gate, Ndurumo secured the chicken coop. With the animals settled for the night, Baba returned to his thingira, where he now lived alone since he ran off Nyambura.

Njerũ and Ndurumo went to nyũmba, a father-free sanctuary, and sat by the fire to wait for supper. Relieved their crime was behind them, their fear briefly vanished. Fear had gripped them when Baba came to help corral the goats. The fear spiked whenever he came close, as if he could sense the fear or read their minds.

But Baba, with his keen vulture-like nose, didn't need to read any boy's mind.

*

In Gĩkũyũ custom, a wife's house (nyũmba) was her domain and her children and any of her female friends or relatives that might visit. The husband never entered nyũmba except after their children were grown, left the house, and established their own households, or in an emergency.

Now, an emergency had occurred at Baba's homestead.

He appeared at nyũmba's threshold.

In a split second, the boys scattered.

Ndurumo dashed into Mother's bedroom and stood squeezed in a corner, close to some old hanging clothes.

Baba rushed after him into the pitch-dark room and felt the walls, corners, and the hanging clothes.

At one point, he touched Ndurumo's shirt. Ndurumo held his breath and stilled his body. Baba mistook his shirt for the hanging clothes and moved on. Unfamiliar with Mother's bedroom, he groped around and tripped on things. He soon gave up and headed back to the living area.

Ndurumo's mind went into overdrive. He recalled what had happened to him and Wairimũ-big because of the pedigree goat. He feared a similar fate awaited him. How long could he remain hidden? Mother would soon light her lantern when darkness eased in. Developments in the living area distracted him from his worrisome thoughts. Instead, he listened.

From my parents' exchanges, he learned Njerũ had clambered up like a monkey and hidden where humans dared not tread, a feat that would remain unbroken in my family. He put up with the heat and smoke, determined to wait it out, perhaps believing our parents were sane enough not to follow him up there.

But when Baba returned to the living area and started looking around, Mother chimed in. "Njerũ went up in itara," (firewood storage bed over the fire pit).

Baba went outside and armed himself with an armful of pieces of firewood from the pile Mother kept under the eaves.

Back inside, he dropped the pile on the floor and flung one piece at a time onto the itara.

By then, Mother had risen from her seat and stood by to watch.

Njerũ choked from the heat and smoke, but the assault of the firewood overwhelmed him.

He jumped down the seven feet and landed in a heap by the door.

Before he recovered to scuttle through the exit, Baba grabbed his shirt. Instead of checking whether his son suffered broken bones, as a normal father would do, Baba started his free-for-all assault.

He slammed, slapped, roughed, and beat his thirteen-year-old as if the two were in a no-rules wrestling match.

At the height of Baba's insanity, Ndurumo shot out of the bedroom like an arrow. Mother, standing by like a referee, got spooked and yelped when he ran into her and almost knocked her to the floor.

As soon as Ndurumo cleared the threshold, he rounded the house to the back, stood under the eaves, and perked his ears.

As the beating intensified, Njerũ's body went into survival mode. He stopped crying, screaming, or trying to get away. He lay there and took the blows.

"Baba, you're beating me as if I'm a grown man you are fighting with," Njerũ said, a line Mother and others later repeated many times, and which might have saved Njerũ.

"On hearing this," Ndurumo told me, "I cried."

After fifty-seven years, Ndurumo still choked up as he told me that story. Njerũ's beating must have affected him more because he never choked when he told me about his own beating during the pedigree goat incident.

Mother told us the orange assault story in my teens and again in my adulthood. She blamed Baba for going too far with his punishments. My siblings and I never said we knew she told on Njerũ.

To her credit, she never reported my brothers to Baba again. Instead, she dealt with their infractions on her own, with a whack here and a pinch there, but mainly with her vocal mouth.

None of us wanted to hear her loud mouth, especially when we moved to the village, and she did not mind who heard her reprimanding us.

She also never threatened us with, "Wait until your father comes home," a warning I later heard many abused and powerless mothers use and still use.

State of Emergency

26 The Exodus

The freedom I enjoyed, which shaped my earliest childhood memories of my mother when I accompanied her to her job or to our garden, lasted only six months before our lives changed.

Mother talked about an emergency. I had heard Chũchũ Nyandia say the same thing four months earlier when she came to see baby Macharia.

What did it mean? I noticed no changes in our family.

I later learned that men known as Mau Mau had rebelled against the colonial government and taken up arms to fight for the return of the community's seized lands and independence. To calm European settlers' jitters and to protect them from the peasant Gĩkũyũ population—and Mau Mau members in particular—the colonial Governor, Sir Evelyn Baring, declared a state of emergency in the entire country on October 21, 1952.

The previous day, the government had arrested Jomo Kenyatta and a group of 129 Gĩkũyũ political activists, including a handful of non-Gĩkũyũ supporters (and subsequently thousands of others), and transported them to various detention camps.

The authorities never told the men where they were taking them until the so-called dissidents arrived at the Lokitaung and Lodwar detention camps in arid northern Kenya. Those became their torture and hard labor centers for seven of the leaders for the next seven years. Bildad Kaggia, who would later write Roots of Freedom 1921-1963, stayed in for nine years.

Then the colonial government led the country's largest exodus. They first mobilized the Gĩkũyũ tribe—men, women, and children—and transported them to secure villages in the native reserve, on colonial farms, or segregated them in town neighborhoods. The government sent to concentration or detention camps those they accused or claimed supported or affiliated with the Mau Mau.

During the exodus, the first sign that something was odd was the noisy activity I noticed from a family behind our homestead.

"The lorry is here!" a man shouted.

"The lorry has arrived!" others echoed.

I heard rumbling noises, perhaps my first vehicle sound. Longing to see what they referred to, I inched outside the gate. The commotion grew when the lorry, already full of people, stopped a short distance behind Baba's thingira. A man, a woman, and their friends dashed behind our homestead. They reappeared carrying baskets and two small wooden suitcases.

Nobody took things from nyũmba. That meant my family was not riding in that lorry. Curious, I inched closer. Others did the same, although I don't recall seeing Baba; the episode seemed too much like confusion.

Two men from the lorry got off to help load the luggage. People squeezed in with whatever few belongings they carried. They shifted this and that to fit in while they complained the mzungu—European—should have ordered two lorries for his farm. Women stood at the center of the lorry's bed; others sat on their luggage to protect it from hurried or careless feet. Some mothers hushed their screaming babies, holding them to their chests with ngoi and cloths; others comforted children on their laps or beside them.

Men lined the periphery, younger ones in old work trousers under untucked shirts. Some wore hats, their sandaled right feet firmly on the lorry's edge, hands tightened around the sidebars of the canopy-less lorry.

The lorry took off like a getaway car before the passengers settled in. A hat flew off one man's head. He flailed his arms to catch it, but he stopped when another man asked him whether he wanted to fly away like his hat.

Months later, when we moved to the village, and I grew older and understood what was going on, I learned that, just like the lorry that came to Kĩrĩma-inĩ, other lorries had made several trips along Solai Road to pick up people who waited in designated spots.

Unfortunately for Werũ, the bonus son, and his young bride, Ruth, their time together was limited, a payoff for not taking the earlier lorry.

While they waited for theirs by the roadside with others, they saw Alan, at a distance, hurrying toward them, his arms swinging—an unusual behavior for his mild nature.

"That's my father," Ruth said. "I hope nothing is wrong."

"We'll know soon enough," Werũ replied.

By the time Alan reached them, he was breathing heavily and spared no energy for explanations.

"Take your luggage and head home right now," he said to his daughter, thrusting his index finger toward her and then homeward.

"I leave my husband?" Ruth asked, her eyes wide, puzzled, and embarrassed.

"You aren't going to that native reserve!"

Ruth pouted and fought off tears.

Werũ became stupefied and said nothing.

"Now!" Alan ordered.

Ruth picked up her small wooden suitcase and turned her back on her husband, likely hoping she could smuggle herself on a later ride.

Werũ went to the roadside as a married man and rode on the exodus lorry wife-less and depressed. However, that was a minor hiccup compared to what awaited him—a turmoil that would choke him and the country for years.

Kaguyu's other two children did not join in the exodus. Gathoni, the second daughter, remained with her husband and infant daughter in Subukia, where she still lives today.

The youngest son, Gĩthũi-big, left with Aunt Julia in 1945. By the time of the exodus, he lived with Ishmael Gĩchũhĩ, Aunt Julia's long-term boyfriend, and his family in Mũrang'a County, where he attended elementary and middle schools.

Except for their mother, Kaguyu, none of the family members who joined the exodus had ever visited their destination, the so-called Native Reserve.

In my teens, I learned that Kamunge, like the other European farmers, had handpicked the employees who would remain on the farm. He included my half-brother Waigwa, a man of a calm disposition, who followed rules and needed no supervision.

To remain on the farm, however, the handpicked employees had to put thumbprints (gũthecha kĩrore); most people could not write. This meant signing a loyalty agreement stating that, no matter the outcome of the Mau Mau uprising, the employee would remain loyal and defend the farm.

Waigwa and his half-brother, Werũ, refused to sign. Kamunge enticed Waigwa, offering him the job of overseer when Baba retired, many years later. Kamunge also promised to protect loyal employees from harassment by the colonial government or the Mau Mau.

Waigwa remained adamant and insisted on leaving. Kamunge asked Baba to intervene.

Baba happily did. He preferred his son to remain as well. Except for Mother, a woman, Waigwa was the only grown, stable relative Baba could count on.

"Are you sure you want to leave?" Baba asked Waigwa.

"Yes, I cannot sign those papers."

"Weigh the matter carefully," Baba said. "There is too much turmoil going on."

"I don't want to remain tied to Kamunge like a wife."

Waigwa, like his brother Werũ, bet on a Mau Mau win. The idea and prospect of independence, and of people getting their lands back from the British, intoxicated him.

Besides, the family had a head start because Njerũ-big, their oldest brother, and his wife had already moved to Nyeri several years before the war broke out.

As for Baba, he felt relieved after Kaguyu left. Based on a Gĩkũyũ saying that mũtumia wĩ mwana ndateyagwo (a wife with a child is never divorced), if Kaguyu stayed in Solai, people would still have referred to her as Warama's senior wife.

So Baba welcomed the added distance. Besides, by the time of the exodus, he had had enough of polygamy and had settled down with Mother. I doubt he wanted to meddle with that stability.

I also doubt Mother sacrificed a tear to see Kaguyu leave. She strutted around the courtyard as if she were the senior wife. She needed no reminder that she had come in second after Kaguyu.

Kaguyu could not have minded, either. Despite her divorce from Baba, distance did not mean absence. Though banished behind the compound, Kaguyu and her children remained under his authority. His temper still reached them. Years later, I learned his violence knew no bounds. For the second time, he tied teenage Wairimũ-big to a post and beat her for leaving the goats with Ndurumo and going to church with her friends.

Waigwa grew tired of the violence. He moved his mother and sister to Werũ's house, who was away working at Bahati. Before Werũ returned, Waigwa asked Kamunge for permission to build his own homestead at Gathũmbĩ's. He started by building a small house for his mother and sister. So, after a stormy, broken thirty-year marriage, Kaguyu preferred to return to Nyeri, among her people, where she was born and raised.

We—Baba's second family—had no choice. We remained behind because he had sworn when he left Nyeri that, war or peace, his family would never return to the native reserve if he had any say.

Still, our lives changed.

27. The Political Winds

My siblings and I were born in Solai, Nakuru County, at the bottom of the Rift Valley; our lives intertwined with the land stretched across those colonial farms. According to family lore, Baba's lineage traced back to Embu—a connection reflected in the names of his father, Njerũ, and his grandfather, Njagĩ— though these ties dated back to an obscure and distant past.

Otherwise, my parents and their ancestors came from Nyeri, under the shadow of the sacred, snow-capped Mount Kenya. In those days, before its peaks began to lose their white crowns, the mountain stood in quiet majesty, shaping the lives of people, animals, and crops. Because of its temperate climate, the Agĩkũyũ called Nyeri the land of milk and honey. The community spoke of four seasons, the coldest known as *Muoria Nyoni*— the one that freezes birds—when some were said to stiffen on the branches where they perched.

Now, living at Kirima-ini, a wooded homestead set apart from neighbors and settled into the rhythms of the colonial farm, my parents had little access to political news. With no radio and only rumors carried by the landowner or through hearsay, they never expected drastic changes in their lives. But it was bound to happen. Their fellow natives, who knew better, could endure a life without self-determination only for so long.

The older generation still nursed nightmares. They had passed on the history of life before the invasion to the younger generation. They remembered when ethnic communities in Kenya and elsewhere in Africa had their own ancestral homelands, with self-governing micronations.

In Kenya, we know today, the Maasai, the Luo, the Agĩkũyũ, the Kisii, and the Kamba nations (to name just five of Kenya's 42 tribes) lived under their own self-rule.

These relatively small nations had distinct cultures, clearly defined by their entertainments, foods, languages, legal systems, traditions, legends, and religious myths and superstitions.

For centuries, the micronations interacted, traded, and waged wars—mainly livestock raids—among themselves. Without advanced weapons, however, they never devastated each other as Asians, Europeans, and other nations did in their homelands.

Pre-invasion, the micronations had intricate governance systems that rivaled those of any modern religious, social, or legal system, at least in the Agĩkũyũ system.

Why, then, were their economies not advanced like the Westerners, one would ask? One primary reason was the pleasant climate. The micronations had no pressing ulterior motive or inclination to tie their existence to imperial ambitions or the desire to seize land and rule over others. They therefore had not formed lasting alliances or collaborated with their neighbors on a large scale.

For this reason, the micronations lacked industrial capitalism and majestic structures before the colonizers descended on them.

The scramble for Africa: Foreigners, including Portuguese and Arab traders and enslavers, had trickled in but had confined themselves to Africa's coasts. European explorers, followed by missionaries, the harbingers, were the first to tackle the interior.

Then, in 1884, representatives of European powers met in Berlin, Germany, to discuss Africa. They represented Britain, Germany, France, Belgium, Italy, the Netherlands, and Portugal. They agreed on the best way to slice Africa into spheres of influence and conquer the continent, which they dubbed "The Dark Continent" because they knew little about it. To this day, Africa still shoulders the burden of the "dark continent" label. As Paul Bohannan notes in *Africa and Africans:*

"Africa has, for generations now, been viewed through a web of myth so pervasive and so glib that understanding it becomes a twofold task: the task of clarifying the myth and the separate task of examining whatever reality has been hidden behind it. Only as it is stated and told can the myth be stripped away. Only if the myth is stripped away can the reality of Africa emerge."

Whatever the case, a year later, in 1885, the European representatives returned to Berlin and formalized their agreement.

They were then ready to tackle and unravel the "Dark Continent" through what they later labeled "The Scramble for Africa." They descended on Africa like vultures on roadkill.

The British descended on Kenya. They conquered the various micro-nations, one by one, from Mombasa on the Indian Ocean to Lake Victoria to the west. The micronations resisted and fought back (Taita Taveta reportedly took eight years to conquer). But their resistance was no match for the British because:

• Of their superior gunpowder weaponry that their empire had unleashed on humankind

• They were a bigger, stronger nation

• Of local collaborators and traitors like Karŭri wa Gakure; Masaku wa Munyati (also known as Masaku wa Muteo), after whom Machakos is named; Nabongo Mumia, after whom the town of Mumias is named; and others. These were men whom the British recruited and raised to positions of prominence to help suppress the uprisings and later to oppress and contain the masses.

One story I heard as a young girl was of a Gĩkũyũ leader, Waiyaki wa Hinga.

In 1890, he allowed Captain (later Lord) Frederick Lugard to build a post on behalf of the Imperial British East Africa Company (IBEAC). The two men took an oath—a solemn, binding pledge to the Gĩkũyũ community—that Captain Lugard's free use of the land was temporary. But Captain Lugard did not intend to respect the oath.

By 1892, relations had deteriorated to the point of being unbearable. From the community's accounts, his porters harassed the natives, looted their goats, raped their women, and devastated the Gĩkũyũ community so they would vacate and abandon their lands, a practice that the colonial government would apply over and over.

In retaliation, the natives burned down Lugard's outpost to eject him.

Besides seizing the landowners' lands, the IBEAC representatives arrested Waiyaki, took him to Taita Taveta County, and buried him alive, upside down, in an unmarked grave. The shock and trauma within the Gĩkũyũ community became so deep that they have passed that story on from one generation to the next.

Reordering a Nation: Initially, Britain designated Kenya as a protectorate in 1895 to secure its interests after the IBEAC failed to manage the territory. They desired to control trade routes, gain access to resources, and maintain influence in competition with other European powers.

In other words, they took over the administration to enforce a more formal control, including laying the groundwork for the infrastructure they needed, establishing white settlements, and protecting explorers and missionaries from the native population, which was determined to drive the intruders out. Meanwhile, the foreigners wrote back home about the unmolested continent, ready for discovery, settlement, and "civilization."

In time, Kenya's doors opened to all and sundry. More missionaries, fortune-seekers, speculators, charlatans, and hoodlums arrived to spread their afterlife beliefs, lay claim, make a quick shilling, or avoid prosecution and start life anew.

To these conquerors, one black skin looked the same as the next. When they descended upon their spoils and established their new colonies and protectorates, they did not concern themselves with which micro-nation owned what land. They drew arbitrary boundaries and clustered citizens—now called tribes—into a hodgepodge of larger countries. They even split micronations between countries under different colonial masters.

For example, in Kenya, the British split the Luo nation between Kenya and Uganda; the Maasai between Kenya and Tanzania; and the Somalis between Kenya and Somalia.

The Kenya/Somalia split turned out to be the worst. After Kenya attained independence from Britain on December 12,

1963, Somalia demanded the strip of land that Kenyan Somalis occupied, with the intention of uniting the formerly split community. The disagreement escalated into the Shifta War of the 1960s.

Although the war ended without a change in boundaries, the split remains a thorn in Kenya's northern border.

Because of its central location, the Gĩkũyũ nation did not get split. Instead—because it comprised fertile temperate lands—the British crushed its citizens' uprising, torched their homes, killed hundreds, and seized their farmlands. The invaders then crammed the people into a smaller area, now termed the native reserve, similar to Native American reservations in the United States.

They designated the largest portion as White Highlands, where only whites could live and own land. Africans could live there only as domestic workers or farm laborers. The rest became Crown Lands—meaning they now belonged to England.

Missionaries received large tracts of land. The Church of Scotland Mission and the Consolata Mission built permanent stations. In my home area of Solai, where my father migrated in the 1920s, the Anglican (Episcopal) Church dominated. The neighboring Major Stein's farm, where my cousins lived, belonged to the Catholics.

Life Under the New System: By the close of the 1890s, the colonizers had identified their initial priorities for their new order. They needed a railway line to transport goods such as tea, coffee, and pyrethrum from the interior to Mombasa. Cheap labor from India, then a British colony, completed construction of the railway from Mombasa to Kisumu on Lake Victoria in 1901.

The colonizers "upgraded" Kenya to a British colony nineteen years later, in 1920. With the colony under control, the new rulers organized Kenya under the English power structure. The British became the landowners and decision-makers, while Kenyans became their workers and British subjects. Grown men, including former heads and pillars of their communities, became mere "boys."

Meanwhile, the colonial administrators enforced British laws—some copied from the draconian slave systems in the Americas and apartheid in South Africa. The missionaries helped greatly by bringing formal education to Kenya and other parts of Africa. However, they also maligned, suppressed, and shredded African religions, replacing them with Christianity—and in the process, unraveling the names, languages, and traditions that formed the fabric of the people, the effects of which I doubt can ever be erased.

Africans, like my father, became disoriented. He had witnessed the invasion mayhem as a child. By his teens, the invaders had thrown the natives into a new system that had obliterated everything they knew.

To operate in the new government, men left their homelands—now designated native reserves—and their families (who would join them later or not at all) to seek jobs in towns or on European farms.

That was how my family ended up in Kĩrĩma-inĩ. And as I soon learned, even that was temporary. I would not grow up there.

28. Kabati

The political winds soon reached our homestead.

Not long after the exodus lorry left, I heard Mother say Kamunge wanted his employees to live close together, not scattered all over the farm. He wanted them where he could keep an eye on them, to protect them from the alleged Mau Mau "terrorists."

I did not know what that meant or that it included my family until the commotion I saw during the lorry ride started in our homestead. I then understood why Baba had been arriving at dusk. As I soon learned, he was building another homestead for us.

One Sunday, he and two men dismantled our granary and carried big posts on their shoulders.

Then came the moving time. Mother packed and carried on her back piles and piles of our household effects. It took her several days to finish. Nyandia and I, at six and four, were too young to help her with female chores. But I may have helped carry baby Macharia on our last day at Kĩrĩma-inĩ, I'm not sure.

I don't even know what happened to our houses; we just walked away.

When we arrived at Kabati, about two or three miles away, we found our new cottages' muddy walls were still damp, and fresh grass-thatch had streaks of green. Two women were on the roof finishing thatching my mother's hovel. The two cottages had no inside partitions. With scrubby vegetation around, the place looked like a campsite in the middle of the savanna.

I never remember much about that place. Besides the flash of our arrival, my memory is stuck on Mother seated on a low bench on one side of the fire pit, Macharia in her lap. She complained about the hurried move, the lack of room for the family and animals, and about moving into a shack unfit for human habitation.

"The dampness will cause my children to catch pneumonia," she said. Another time I heard her say, "The dampness will kill my children."

She especially worried about the youngest ones—Macharia at six months and Gĩthũi at two-and-a-half years old. Mother did not complain about the fireplace. We had three new and sturdier masonry stones she had scavenged at the quarry. They could support a sizable pot without the danger of tipping over.

Besides the moving activity, Mother fetched food, cooked, and cared for her family. By the time she left her job or the garden, with baby Macharia on her back or front, arrived home and kindled the fire, it was late afternoon.

Saddled with an infant while her hungry brood's little eyes focused on her, Mother hurried to cook supper. She worked from dawn until bedtime. But she took it in stride because, according to her, njogu ndĩremagwo nĩ mĩguongo yayo (an elephant is never defeated by its tusks).

But one day, one of her tusks rattled her when pressure peaked, causing her to suffer a second's worth of insanity and turn into a crazed fire thrower.

It started with the death of a chicken. When Mother arrived home late Saturday afternoon, she boiled a big pot of water. She told my older brothers—Njerũ, Ndurumo, and Machira—to catch a certain chicken for slaughter, no doubt after she sought Baba's permission.

My brothers cherished that kind of task not only because they were going to eat a delicacy but also because they enjoyed chases, especially sanctioned ones. Baba in his thingira—well, in his temporary shack then—would not click his tongue and ask, "What's that racket all about?"

So my brothers dashed this and that, shrieking while the terrified chickens, not knowing who would be the victim, rushed, squawked, and flapped their wings. When the chosen one got snared, their squawks trailed off, and they turned to watch one of their own taken away.

When one brother handed the chicken to Mother, she clasped its wings at the shoulders with one hand like handcuffs. With the other hand, she held its legs along with a knife she had sharpened on a file Baba kept in his thingira.

The poor chicken squawked and squawked as Mother marched behind the cottage. Curious and eager to witness our first slaughter, Nyandia and I followed at a distance, while Gĩthũi toddled behind us.

Mother laid the chicken on its side in a grassy area. She stepped on its clamped wings with one foot and on the legs with the other. She held the chicken's head, clasped its beak to stop its cries, and raised her arm, knife in hand. With the chicken quiet, she became aware of our presence, raised her head, and saw us.

"Go back to your play," she said.

We trotted back to the front.

In no time, Mother emerged, dangling the chicken by its legs, head halfway cut, blood still oozing from the neck wound with an occasional drip.

In all my six years, I had not witnessed a single slaughter. That day, I connected our meat and its source. Subsequently, whenever Mother or Baba slaughtered a hen or a goat, they did so out of our sight. If we rushed to see, they shooed us away as if they did not want us to witness them killing an animal.

In the house, Mother removed the pot of boiling water from the fire. She dunked the chicken into the hot water, then held the legs and turned the chicken from one side to the other, pausing between the rolls to ensure the hot water loosened the feathers without peeling the skin. Whenever she turned the chicken, a gush of hot steam flared and assaulted our little faces.

"Stand back!" Mother said. "This can burn you."

We stood back, wiped the moisture from our faces, and claimed we could handle it before we closed in to gawk again.

Mother scooped hot water with a white mug and poured it over the knees that she could not submerge. When she determined the feathers were loose enough, she pulled the chicken out and rested it on a tin basin.

When it cooled somewhat, my brothers helped pluck it. They pulled fistfuls of feathers and finally picked out the tiniest hairs around the knees and the neck. Mother then turned the carcass over a flame that zapped the tiny pin-hairs that fingers couldn't grab and pluck.

To cut the chicken, she opened the stomach, removed the innards, saved the gizzard to clean later, and put the rest aside for the cat. She discarded the head and the feet, parts that we later learned some people ate.

Mother sautéed green leafy onions in oil and browned the chunks of chicken. She added salt before she added enough water to cover the chunks. She also put fresh firewood into the fire from all three sides of the fire pit.

Whoever held baby Macharia, most likely Njerũ or Ndurumo, handed him back to Mother after she settled back in her seat. She put him on her lap. The rest of us children huddled around the other two sides of the fire.

"Don't get too close," Mother said. "I don't want to end up with a scorched child."

We chattered, watched, and waited for the chicken to cook.

Meanwhile, Ndurumo had claimed the chicken's stomach as he, Njerũ, or Machira did whenever Mother slaughtered a chicken. Because darkness had set in, he cleaned it indoors and made himself a balloon.

He stood on one side of the cottage and blew air into the balloon. Whenever he let go, the balloon snapped, air popped out, and it sailed overhead, clear across the room. In one instance, however, instead of flying, the balloon smacked POW! right into the bubbling soup. Hot splashes and droplets sprayed in every direction.

Njerũ and Machira howled and shot to their feet.

We, little children, fell back. Nyandia or Gĩthũi ended up on the floor. We shrieked and cried while we wiped our faces and finally got on our feet.

Mother half spun away from the fire to shield Macharia.

The second droplets stopped flying, she spun back toward the fire.

"He will burn my children!" she said as she whipped out a piece of blazing firewood and hurled it at Ndurumo.

Thunk!

Ndurumo ducked in a mere second.

The wood made a dent in the wall where he had stood. It missed him by inches, while it scattered hundreds of sparks that enveloped him. They almost set his shirt ablaze.

Mother's reaction clamped shut every mouth and sound in the room except for the crackling fire and the bubbling soup.

Even when we settled back, we controlled our usual racket while we waited for supper. Even Mother's demeanor changed; she spoke in a softer tone.

When she served us our food, we controlled how much we smacked our mouths so as not to disturb the peace. Mother, like me, sneaked glances at Ndurumo. She did not ask him to hold the baby or help with anything else that evening.

Besides Mother's complaints about dampness, the chicken incident remains my only clear memory of our stay at Kabati.

After just four months, another commotion descended on our temporary camp. Mother started packing again and loading bales onto her back. Mũthũngũ nĩarerichũkirwo (the European changed his mind), she said.

At six and a half years old, I knew my parents worked for mũthũngũ, but I didn't connect him to the "skinless" man I had seen at Mother's job.

Four months earlier, when we started moving from Kĩrĩma-inĩ, I thought it was part of our lives. But when Mother said the European changed his mind at Kabati, I got the feeling that the person she and my father worked for somehow controlled what we did. But this didn't crystallize until various changes occurred in the village.

For now, Kamunge, the European, had ordered my family to move yet again.

29. The Village

We moved into a village at a higher elevation, four miles east of Kabati. It contained about a hundred mud and thatch, new and old, circular houses, most in clusters around small courtyards.

A close-knit chain-link and barbed wire fence, nine to ten feet high, with several rows of slanted barbed wire along the top, similar to a prison's, surrounded the village. A ditch several feet deep ran along the outside of the fence. Like a castle moat, it ensured no person could breach the fence from the inside or outside. Parents did not have to watch their children or warn them. Even adventurous Machira, who embraced life fully, ignored that fence.

People entered or left the village through the foot gate to the east that was guarded by a non-Gĩkũyũ.

Although our adopted homestead was smaller than Kĩrĩma-inĩ, it looked similar, except it had no goats' cottage. I later learned that Mr. Nyaga, Kamunge's cook, who was married to

Waigwa's sister-in-law and who left on the exodus lorry, had occupied the homestead. Perhaps he didn't need a cottage for a few goats.

Baba built one for his goats with the help of others.

Just like Kĩrĩma-inĩ, the homestead faced northwest, and thingira, its back to the village, commanded the best view of the courtyard.

We entered from the side between thingira and nyũmba. If people entered our courtyard, we couldn't see them if we were in thingira or nyũmba. We saw them only when we were outdoors. We got alerted when a person reached the threshold. However, except for children, adults did not sneak in on us. Right from the entrance, they cleared their throats, faked a cough or grunt, or asked whether anyone was home.

Until we arrived in the village, my parents may not have known that, after the colonial governor declared a state of emergency, Kamunge wanted us out of our secluded homestead at Kĩrĩma-inĩ without further delay. He intended for us to stay temporarily at Kabati only until he got the village fenced and the last shipment of people to the native reserve vacated the older houses.

When we arrived, goats and chickens loitered about with no one to restrict their movement. When evening came, each animal gravitated toward its regular home. And personal effects remained intact in the houses.

In nyũmba, the house Mother adopted, we found, besides household items, pots, pans, trays, and baskets full of roasted goat meat and other cooked foods. Without knowing where their next meal would come from, the people flagged for the exodus intended to carry food with them. They learned they couldn't do so on the day of their departure.

The families who moved into other abandoned homesteads adopted the animals, kept the household effects, and ate whatever food they found. For the first and last time, women enjoyed cook-free days before they prepared meals for their families.

But no such luck for my mother.

Baba, a loyal and perfect model of the colonized, viewed everything people left behind with disdain as if it were tainted or taboo. He forbade my family from eating the food or using the items.

Instead, he and my brothers dug a big hole near the fence, into which he ordered Mother and my brothers to dump the meat and other food. He and the boys covered the grave as one would for the dead.

Baba let the goats and chickens spend the night, chickens in their coop, and goats settled in the periphery by the houses' eaves. The next day, with the help of my brothers and a handful of men, he rounded them up, gathered the household effects, and delivered them to Kamunge.

I never learned what Kamunge did with the belongings. But it is safe to assume he sold the animals and told his workers to destroy the personal effects, which I suspect they kept for themselves instead.

The two cats we found didn't need anyone's help. They turned feral and lived freely ever after. Well, not really. They must have realized that too much freedom was too burdensome and unfulfilling. In need of a family of their own, they gingerly trailed back in and became part of our household.

Except for blurs, I remember little of this part of the story. For clarity, I relied on the stories my family shared as I grew older. Otherwise, at six and a half years old, my only focus and comfort amidst the uncertainty and all the changes was my mother's presence. But so many houses clustered together fascinated me, and I looked forward to playing with the children who lived there.

For my three older brothers, however, as they later told the story, they noticed the most enticing display of food they had ever seen or would see in all their formative years. They never forgot a single detail well into their senior years.

Even our mother had marveled at Baba's actions.

"How could he be against waste?" she asked, "And turn around and demand such wastage?"

But no one dared question the Great One.

It now puzzles me that Mother did not leave some food in her house. Stuck in his thingira, Baba would not have suspected or found out. But that's the state of conditioned minds.

*

Gradually, I learned that the colonial government segregated Agĩkũyũ from other tribes so that those tribes would not get enticed to join the Mau Mau uprising.

Meru, Embu, Tharaka, and Mbeere, smaller tribes and close cousins of the Gĩkũyũ, got sucked into the Mau Mau uprising, and various levels of political activism occurred across many parts of Kenya. But this book is a family and community memoir that focuses on the Gĩkũyũ farmworkers, the worker bees, and Gĩkũyũland, the highlands, the epicenter of the Mau Mau activities.

*

While my family adjusted to village life and I grew older, I overheard subdued conversations about the Mau Mau uprising. Mother said people feared an informant would overhear them. No one wanted such gossip to reach Kamunge for fear he would label them Mau Mau sympathizers. Such an accusation would have ended with a police interrogation and a likely trip to the feared concentration camps, a place where detainees never knew they would ever come out alive or not.

I did not bother to eavesdrop on Baba. He never indulged in useless talk.

But from the bits of what I heard from the women, I figured Mau Mau members were outlaws who wanted to ruin our lives. For this reason, Kamunge moved us to a camp-like fenced village for our own safety.

My parents and other villagers may have understood Mau Mau's aspirations. But the thought of ejecting the British seemed insurmountable, like a community in a tug-of-war with a god.

The oppression they had endured their entire lives had wiped ideas of ownership and self-determination from their minds. They did not see themselves in any other way except as Kamunge's laborers and subjects, an inheritance that, at a cellular level, they passed on to their descendants.

They had no option but to hunker down and follow orders. That remained their motto: keep their heads down and raise their children.

At least I know Baba stuck to a flawless work ethic and never wanted Kamunge to question his loyalty. He would have done anything to ensure nothing made Kamunge and his family angry, uneasy, or uncomfortable.

Perhaps his memory of a troubled life under the colonial government from his boyhood, and his reason for abandoning Gĩkũyũland, led him to see Kamunge's farm as a sanctuary. And because he had worked for Kamunge for twenty-five years, he likely underestimated the gravity of the state of emergency.

*

Although it never meant much to us then, we were not Kenyans. According to our colonizers, they were the *real* Kenyans. I heard people talk of the various names Europeans called us: "natives, primitives, savages, barbarians, monkeys, or bloody Africans."

(We called ourselves by our tribal names, or Africans, and occasionally black people. It took decades and living outside Kenya before I referred to myself as a Kenyan.)

From women's talk, I learned or sensed that no matter how loyal and hard the Africans worked, Kamunge and other Europeans still viewed them as despicable human beings.

What pathology would make all-powerful people in charge of everything treat so poorly those who worked so hard for them, including raising their children, cooking and cleaning for them, and making their beds? And to top it all, consider those people—the Africans—inferior beings.

My young mind got confused. I could not figure it out, not even as an adult.

And with the Mau Mau uprising, the colonialists' major thrust was to subdue the Africans, particularly the Gĩkũyũ tribe, and erase from their minds any lofty ideas about freedom, restoration of their land, and civil and human rights.

Meanwhile, as the so-called *primitives* weathered the oppression and indoctrination, their colonizers expected them to believe the poor state they found themselves in proved British superiority.

Their masters impressed on these peasants that the militant Gĩkũyũ men and women, who questioned, challenged, and took to the forests to fight for the restoration of their community's seized lands and independence, were terrorists to be knifed, shot on sight, or bombed.

The bits and pieces I heard about the Mau Mau, amidst our hurried moves and at the village, sounded too complicated for me. But I had realized Kamunge wielded the ultimate power.

That did not bother me because nothing bad happened at our homestead. And wherever we moved, I believed my parents were in charge and would ensure my safety, until that, too, became doubtful.

30. Interrogation

Disruption had become part of our lives. And by the time we reached our third homestead in the fenced village, within a year, the emergency had seeped into our daily rhythms.

My mother talked in haste, rushing to do her chores. As for Baba, he no longer brewed his beer, drank, or sat on his three-legged stool on the porch to admire his animals.

Confined to our courtyard, I remained oblivious to the activities in the village. But because of my parents' behavior, it seemed the entire village kept busy and alert.

Their busyness never concerned me, though. Our household's morning and evening routines remained the same, day in and day out.

I also liked that Baba constructed—wove—a new, permanent cot-like bed on one side of Mother's bedroom for Nyandia and me. The bed came with high sides to prevent us from falling out at night. After the common bedroom entryway, Nyandia and I turned right and climbed into our bed.

The bed's entrance was about two feet high, and for a period before we got the hang of it, Mother helped us climb in.

Every morning when I awoke, I found her by the fireplace making tea and porridge, or getting lunch ready for Baba to carry to work.

Baba and his goats caused their own racket in the courtyard. He always let them out of their cottage. Confined in their thingira all night long, the minute he opened the door, the goats rushed out as if on a race. They stretched, bleated, romped, licked their pink salt rocks, which were a major feature on their manger, and caused most of the outdoor activity. Meanwhile, Baba puttered around before or after his mug of tea, waiting to leave for work. To wake my brothers, he shouted from the courtyard, "Are you still sleeping?" Somehow, they always heard him and hustled out of their thingira.

One morning, however, I awoke and, standing in the doorway, rubbing my eyes, sensed that something was amiss. Mother still busied herself with her morning routine, but I heard no activity in the courtyard. Baba would never let the goats remain locked up in daylight.

"Where is Baba?" I asked.

"He'll be back soon," Mother said.

"Where did he go?" my younger siblings and I wanted to know.

"Kũhũngwo mahũri," Mother said.

"What does 'to get interrogated' mean?"

"It's how the government catches wrongdoers."

"Is Baba a wrongdoer?" we asked in chorus.

"Oh! No! It's just a formality," came the reply.

I had heard whispers of the interrogations while we were all settling in, but the word meant nothing to me then. Only with Baba's disappearance did it take on an unsettling turn.

The villagers had not dared to question the order when Kamunge told them about the colonial government's mandated "screening" for every Gĩkũyũ adult—they had no choice. Yet a collective confusion lingered; they had already signed loyalty agreements, binding them to the farm regardless of the war's outcome. Now, the government intended to interrogate them like common criminals? Kamunge knew they were loyal. Why, then, had he not secured their exemption?

According to Mother, Baba—as the loyal overseer—had expected Kamunge to shield him. He was mistaken. He was among the first to be hauled away.

Now, Mother's explanation of "formality" settled me for the day. But that evening felt empty, odd. Our entire household felt different in a bad way. He had always come home after work.

That evening, Mother cooked in thingira while we huddled around the fire, seated on the floor or low benches, subdued.

As days stretched to two, three, and more, malaise descended on our homestead. Based on our visceral fear of Baba, one would think we would want him gone. Instead, his absence had affected all of us; we did not play as boisterously as before.

Although it meant little to me then, we soon learned the colonial government had set up interrogation sites all over Gĩkũyũland—Nyeri, Mũrang'a, and Kĩambuu—and on European farms in the Rift Valley and in towns' neighborhoods where Gĩkũyũ people lived.

The site for our area was at Lambert's farm in neighboring Subukia, about eight miles from our village.

Every week, Kamunge selected about eight individuals. At night, after the village slept, the police sneaked in and hauled them away.

*

Baba endured the "formality" for about eight days. I learned of his return when Mother took him a mug of tea one early morning. He ignored his goats and other activities and stayed home; the only time I saw him miss work.

He remained in his thingira for three days.

After Mother sniffed around for news, she learned that Baba had suffered a "higher level" of interrogation than necessary because "Your father is very stubborn," she said.

The report also said that, no matter the punishment, he insisted he had not taken the oath. The authorities finally had to let him go.

News of Baba's torture threw me off.

If he was not a wrongdoer, as Mother claimed, I asked myself why the government punished him. I doubted Mother's statement that it was "only a formality."

Before that, my overhearing adult conversations was incidental. But after I realized Mother was not forthcoming, I eavesdropped and picked scraps of information whenever an adult dropped by our homestead.

The level of abuse or torture detainees suffered depended on whether the interrogators deemed them innocent, oath-takers, or involved with Mau Mau activities.

Torture ranged from insults, shoves, slaps, and whippings to a dip into a python pit. Also, men suspected of Mau Mau affiliations suffered sleep deprivation, solitary confinement, and torture of private parts until they confessed.

Interrogators applied these so-called "milder" methods of torture to Agĩkũyũ, who remained on European farms. Most of those the colonial government had moved to the native reserves or thrown into crowded detention camps would later report the horrors they endured and suffered, both men and women, including permanent disabilities of mind and limbs, castrations, and deaths.

*

Mother left for the screening camp two weeks after Baba returned to work. Although we did not know when she would go, she had prepared us.

She said not to worry if we woke up one morning and found her gone, because "I won't be gone for long."

But that did not comfort me when I woke up and, while I rubbed my eyes to clear sleep-eye-gunk, I noticed my brother Ndurumo, at thirteen, stirring porridge, seated on Mother's usual spot. A whiff of panic hit me, and my world shattered. I had never woken up and not found my mother busy with her morning chores.

What would I do without her? Everything in my life revolved around my mother, from when I woke up and found breakfast ready to when she cooked supper while my siblings and I waited around the fire.

Mother's best friend, Wanjeri, came to bring water and help Ndurumo cook supper for us. She left early to cook supper for her own children. Ndurumo did the rest. Looking back, he did most of the work, including dealing with four children, all younger than him.

But his efforts and Wanjeri's mattered little to me. They did not shield me from experiencing bouts of sadness. A sharp stub of sorrow that struck me from time to time, and my little chest contracted, growing worse as evening approached.

We did whatever Ndurumo asked of us, but we moved slowly, acted subdued, and seemed out of sorts. I kept asking myself what would happen to me if Mother never returned. I could not think of an answer besides emptiness.

A few months shy of seven, I was like the little birds huddled in a nest waiting for their mother to return and dump food down their throats.

I became so involved with my plight that I do not recall a single incident with my younger siblings during our mother's absence. For the first time, I felt helpless, weighed down by an invisible force, a power stronger than my father.

My anguish because of Mother's absence, however, did not mean I cared less for Baba. I had felt apprehension when he left, but Mother assured us. And she took care of all our needs. I also believed that, as a man, nothing could prevent him from returning home.

But Mother's absence hurt in different ways. Our home seemed and felt empty—the vacuum I agonized about the most.

To stress me even more, I overheard grown-ups talking of beatings. It sounded terrible, which made me wonder whether government officials were beating my mother. Besides the confusion, I did not understand what that meant. I had forgotten my only spanking at four, and I had yet to witness another beating.

Baba was of no help. Holed up in his thingira to await whatever food Ndurumo and Wanjeri prepared for him, and shaped by men's arm's-length parenting, he seemed unaware of how to ease our fears, explain, or talk about the interrogation—then or ever. His attitude remained firm; he had fulfilled his duty, and nothing would change whether he talked or complained.

What I did not know then was that Baba's silence itself had become another form of obedience.

31. Screening Camp

One morning, I woke up and found Mother seated in her esteemed spot by the fire, as if she had never left. I stared at her, wordless, happy, and yet surprised that she had actually come back—I had feared the worst. She looked the same as always.

"Oh, you have woken," she said as a greeting.

"Hmm," I hummed.

"Ũchũrũ wĩhakuhi kũhĩa," the porridge is almost ready.

She shared brief episodes with us children, but reserved long accounts for her friends. I sat nearby whenever a friend dropped in. Unlike other times, she did not shoo me away if I eavesdropped. It took me a long time to piece together a coherent story because Mother discouraged long social calls. They wasted too much time, she claimed.

In time, however, enough pieces fell into place.

At Lambert's camp, she said, the authorities herded people into a catch-all structure. It's unclear whether she went there, but she ended up in a mud-walled, grass-thatched circular hovel occupied by mothers with children—she had carried baby Macharia with her. She found the women occupants leaning against the wall or sitting on the dirt floor. They jabbered about their separation from their families, the state of emergency, and the best way to endure the camp.

Mother felt her way around for a suitable spot. Not one to dillydally, she joined the conversation.

In case she needed to relieve herself, the woman next to her gave her directions to a lonely tin pail on one side of the unpartitioned cottage.

"Relieve myself in front of people?" she asked.

"Well, it's not like we can see you."

Some women must have already helped themselves to the pail because an awful smell engulfed them. That had to be part of the screening hardships, Mother said later.

Before she left home, she had learned through word of mouth that the colonial government had declared a state of emergency because the Mau Mau *terrorists* had gone to the forest and were fighting the government.

She and her friends spoke of how their stance had made their lives harder. They then lived in so-called *secure villages,* subjected to a dusk-to-dawn curfew, and forced to rush to work and to their gardens. Kamunge's animals, wandering in mile-long and wide pens, enjoyed more freedom of movement than the villagers did.

Now at the camp, detainees exchanged bits of stories and helped Mother connect the political fragments she had gathered through rumors. The women who were better informed said Mau Mau members were freedom fighters led by Dedan Kĩmaathi, who were fighting the British to return the lands they stole from the natives and for Kenya's independence.

Detainees discussed Jomo Kenyatta's activism in Kenya and England, as well as his alleged association with the Mau Mau.

Mother did not know about Kenyatta before then.

A handful of knowledgeable women disagreed that Kenyatta was a Mau Mau collaborator. They explained that the fighters were patriots who had lost faith in the slow, "educated" approach of leaders like Kenyatta. After years of fruitless negotiations with the British over land restoration and civil rights, these patriots felt the constitutional path was a dead end.

Mother wondered how the Mau Mau would accomplish such a monumental task. She grew up on a European farm in Nanyuki, having left Gĩkũyũland as a young girl; life on a colonial farm was all she knew. Without the education to understand the intricacies of such possibilities, she resolved to endure the interrogation and return home to her children.

Before her group left home, the women who had gone before her schooled her in how to conduct herself. They said non-oath-takers suffered as much as the oath-takers. Similar to police interrogations, officials punished, tortured, and insisted a person lied until the person, hoping to get relief, admitted he or she had taken the oath. Her advisers said the trick was to confess before the interrogators beat her senseless. They also said lying did not matter as long as one told their story with conviction.

When Mother's turn came, she had her story ready.

Two underfed, scrawny constables in khaki uniforms and elongated maroon-colored hats fetched and hustled her into a dimly lit cottage. (She likely left Macharia with a colleague.) She found three Gĩkũyũ men dressed in trousers, shirts, and overcoats.

Gĩkũyũ-speaking officials, conversant with Gĩkũyũ traditions, myths, beliefs, and the oath process, conducted those interrogations.

This became crucial during the Mau Mau era when the colonial government classified the Gĩkũyũ community:

The masses whom the colonizers conquered and now destabilized yet again, and herded like sheep into guarded villages in the native reserve or European farms, segregated in towns, or sent to detention camps.

Political activists—educated activists like Jomo Kenyatta, who engaged in and believed in change through newsletter campaigns, rallies, negotiations with the colonizers based on the British constitution, and appeals to English civil society.

The Mau Mau nationalists—a splinter from the Kenyatta group. They got a boost and became a force unto themselves after World War II, when the dejected and misplaced veterans joined their ranks. The group seethed with enthusiasm, choosing to live free or die fighting for their birthright.

If the British could force them to fight and die in the thousands for someone else's country, they could surely fight for their own country, restore lands to their rightful owners, and expel the British from Kenya.

The nationalists complained that the educated elite activists wasted time organizing, negotiating, rubbing shoulders with colonialists, being snubbed, and even traveling to London to "beg for their own lands" in the British parliament.

How could anyone negotiate the return of their own seized and occupied lands in the occupiers' country? Mau Mau members, their supporters, and sympathizers marveled.

The loyalists—the middle-class Christian men educated by the missionaries who sided with, supported, and aided the colonizers.

Through their education and religious affiliations, they educated their children, some of them abroad, and benefited socially and financially through colonialism.

Many senior loyalists owned substantial landholdings, and some had even become surrogate colonizers. Independence for their fellow Africans, therefore, meant more people to share with, which would have jeopardized their privileged lifestyles.

As a result, anyone who opposed or interfered with the colonizers' set hierarchy became an enemy of the loyalists.

After the Mau Mau uprising, the colonial government paid more attention to the loyalists, who already had a stake in the system. They became the colonizers' natural allies, and their power grew exponentially.

The colonial administration promoted them to home guard positions, to chiefs and other senior positions, and gave them subordinates at their disposal. The government backing enabled them and their rank and file to apply whatever heinous methods they could to ensure the Gĩkũyũ masses conformed to the colonial dictates, and that the Mau Mau were defeated and wiped out.

Defectors/the Captured—mid and senior Mau Mau member defectors or those who got captured, and the colonial government spared their lives for their cooperation. Their guerrilla warfare skills and knowledge of Mau Mau's operations and oath made them more valuable alive than dead.

Those were the types of loyalists Mother faced at Lambert's screening camp.

When she went before them, she told them she had never taken Mau Mau or any other oath. Except for basic questions and verbal intimidation, I recall nothing noteworthy she said about that first stage.

In Mother's last session, as before, she denied taking an oath.

"Get your story straight," he said. "Do you mean you don't want your lands back?"

When she stuck to her denial, the man shoved and slapped her. She ended up on the floor.

"I saw stars," she told two women.

"Ah!" one woman said.

"No one has ever slapped me like that, not even my husband."

"As I lay there, an image of my children flashed through my mind. It was the right time to confess. I told them I had taken an oath only once. I talked fast and promised to tell them everything they wanted."

"Get up and sit on that chair," one interrogator told her.

Mother struggled through a barrage of insults. Finally, seated on the wooden chair, one interrogator rained questions on her.

"Describe how you saw the oath administered and how you took it."

Having taken no oath, Mother described the process she saw Baba and other men follow to slaughter goats. She said that the oath administrators instructed her, along with others, to eat raw meat like animals.

"The interrogators had to know I was lying," Mother said to her friends. "I couldn't describe something I had never witnessed."

She told her story so well, she said, that the men thanked her for her "honesty."

Mother returned home on the sixth day, and our house found its rhythm again.

32. Passbooks

At the detention camp, people from the various farms were herded together. They never learned what happened to their village mates until the authorities whisked them into a van for their night trip back home.

Sometimes the officials cleared someone, but the person remained at the camp, likely waiting for colleagues to get processed.

Those cleared also never learned what happened to the ones from the neighboring farms with whom they shared cottages or the catchall barn.

At home, word spread that a handful of male detainees from two of the farms never returned to their families. People said the government must have hustled them into detention camps.

To our relief, my parents and their fellow villagers all came out "clean." But that did not make them feel secure. They could not leave the farm freely; interrogation was only the beginning.

Across the country, the colonial government issued passbooks to Gĩkũyũ males from teenagers to those a step away from the grave. Women traveled as dependents.

Passbooks had columns, like the booklets post offices and banks used to record deposits and withdrawals.

To walk to the market, the clinic, or anywhere else outside the farm, every male from age sixteen had to carry a passbook showing the farm and landowner's names, and his authorization.

"I received a passbook and paid taxes," Ndurumo said, "before I qualified for an ID card."

He walked 20 miles to Nakuru Town four times in two months to get that passbook. The man in charge—a Gĩkũyũ loyalist—subjected Ndurumo to two rigorous interviews because he claimed Ndurumo was not who he claimed he was. At sixteen, born at home and not yet eligible for an ID, he had no proof unless someone with proof could ID him.

Finally, he received his passbook on his fourth trip only because the loyalist was absent that day.

It could have been easier if Baba had taken Ndurumo to Nakuru. But he was a part-time employee, and Kamunge did not want two employees absent.

To Kamunge, Ndurumo could travel and negotiate for his passbook (I doubt he knew Ndurumo had to walk), and work on the farm, but was not mature enough to receive his own wages. Instead of paying him, Kamunge gave it to Baba for safe-keeping, most likely depositing it in Baba's post office account.

During his four trips, Ndurumo had no place to spend the night. Even if he did, he could not take a chance in case a white person or the police stopped him without official travel authorization.

He found it safer to walk back home and duck into the bushes if he heard a car approach.

Ndurumo had reason to get nervous. Every white man in Kenya could stop any African in public and ask for travel papers. If he deemed the papers flawed, he had the legal or implied right to arrest the individual and deliver them to a police station.

(White women could have done the same, but because most of them were dependents, they merely deferred to their husbands.)

Sometimes, European men, mainly farm managers, slapped and kicked the so-called criminals they arrested before taking them to the police station.

Others, like the manager of neighboring Major Stein's farm, where my mother's two uncles and their families lived, did not involve the police. They dished out whatever punishment they deemed fit the "crime," which included physical attacks followed by warnings.

Word reached us that one young man resisted, and he and the manager got into a fistfight.

Those sadistic managers were a terror to young African men.

*

Although my life revolved around my mother long before we moved to the village, and her authority affected me daily, I somehow understood that Baba wielded more power than Mother and had the final say in our household. I believed he owned our homestead, our garden, the open grassland, his goats and chickens, and our belongings.

Then came our hurried move to the barely finished hovels at Kabati and, after four months, on to the fenced village while Mother complained in her usual self-talk. But Baba went along and remained quiet.

Initially, it confused me why he let all those changes happen to us just because Kamunge said so. But I saw and overheard enough in my seventh and eighth years to understand that, although Baba's authority loomed large at our homestead, it did not extend beyond it. He owned little, and what he owned could disappear at the whim of Kamunge or his son, Kang'oro.

It's not that I thought seriously about these matters; some things stuck in my mind because they confused me, and others came to me as an awareness.

The first incident of Baba's limited power crystallized when unknown people came at night like kidnappers and whisked him and my mother away to the screening camp. I then realized with dismay that anything could happen to my family and that Baba lacked the power to prevent it.

*

As my family and others settled into village life and their new reality, including a dusk-to-dawn curfew, news reached us that Kamunge wanted to appoint Baba as a "home guard." My heart swelled with pride.

Even though I did not know the details of a home guard's duties, I was sure the new post would elevate Baba's status.

Years later, I would learn that Baba would have learned to shoot a gun, received a bonus, and would be exempt from the higher taxes charged to regular Gĩkũyũ men.

My siblings and I waited for Baba's big day. None of us expected him to tell us when he got appointed. So, I observed him to see if he displayed any unusual mannerisms. In the interim, if someone mentioned Baba's potential appointment, Mother clicked her tongue and continued with whatever she was doing without comment.

"Your father will be Kamunge's eyes and ears," she said one day after she came from the hydrant outside the gate. She said this with an attitude, working faster, which made the dishes rattle. Someone must have told her something negative about the home guard appointment.

Negative energy oozed from her whenever Mother had no say in a decision Baba made or something beyond her control. Whenever this happened, my siblings and I shut up and stayed out of her way, looking at her cross-eyed now and then.

Now, I wondered why Mother could not be happy for Baba.

But I disliked anybody who talked about me to my parents. So if my father became Kamunge's eyes and ears, he would report people because, unlike Kamunge, he lacked the power to do much else. Then he would not regain or increase his power as I had imagined.

I could not decide which was worse: being a home guard or being powerless.

I did not have to figure it out. We waited and waited, but heard not another word about the home guard position.

Meanwhile, we heard occasional news of the Mau Mau and the colonizers' forces fighting, something that seemed so far away from us.

At one time, a plane dropped leaflets over the village. I picked up one. It showed a black-and-white image of a shirtless, shackled man with dreadlocks, lying on his back, slightly propped up on a bed with white sheets. Without knowing how to read, and not having grown enough to think we could use it for kindling, I tossed it.

News soon trickled down from a few people who could read. They said the image was of the lead Mau Mau terrorist, and the flyers were a warning to those who parleyed or sympathized with the Mau Mau.

Meanwhile, we heard of men who paid fines or went to jail for breaking curfew if the authorities caught them sneaking out of the farm for a quick errand without authorization.

The news did not bother me because it had never happened to my parents. And except for Njerū and Ndurumo, who attended school, and Machira, who went goat herding, the rest of us stayed home.

Sickness & Health

33. Ancestral Healing Hands

While the government tightened its grip on our movements, village life found quieter ways to hold itself together.

Mother adjusted to village life faster than anyone else in our family. She slowed her hectic pace and made friends who helped her when she was absent or sick, like when Wanjeri came to cook for us during her interrogation hiatus. Mama Alan was another woman I considered a friend of my mother, although not a typical socializing friend.

I had not met her yet, but I knew she was old because Mother referred to her with deference, as if she were our special grandmother. She and her husband, Mũgono, were the oldest people in our community. Although they were Agĩkũyũ, Kamunge had allowed them to live outside the village, perhaps because of their advanced age. Without the benefit of books, the couple—particularly Mama Alan, born before the invasion—was a walking library of Gĩkũyũ's old ways, information no one had the foresight, education, or know-how to record.

They also served as surrogate grandparents to the village children, since none of them (except the Alans) had grandparents. Many of them were dead, or a handful had been swept in with the exodus to the native reserve.

Mama Alan flourished in her grandmotherly role, according to rumors that reached me, which later proved true. She also gave free massages to sick children.

But her husband, Mũgono, a stooped, grumpy old man with tufts of thick, woolly hair as white as one of Baba's goats, preferred a quieter life. He did not cherish his grandfather's status, least of all to non-relatives. He directed his energy and respect toward his wife, the conduit between him and their mild-mannered only son, Alan, and his family.

Alan was the man who marched to the lorry stop during the exodus and ordered his daughter Ruth to return home and forget the lorry ride and her husband, Werũ.

Perhaps Alan had taken after his father, Mũgono, who was content to spend his old age in peace. He detested children who caused a ruckus or hung around his two-house homestead, hoping for snacks that Mama Alan occasionally dished out. When he saw the children, he made garbled, guttural grunts. "Get out of here," he said. "Go play elsewhere."

If they didn't take heed fast, he rose from where he basked in the sun, seated on his stool, gathered his long cloth tied on his left shoulder, and shooed them away with his walking stick. "Go away! Get out of here!"

If Mama Alan caught him in the act, she chastised him and said that children visiting a person's homestead was a blessing. He never contradicted her verbally, but he continued his mean ways behind her back.

The day I first met Mama Alan, my brother Macharia had been crying nonstop, no matter what our mother did. She abandoned cooking supper, sang him lullabies such as "Mwaana wiitũ kiira. Kiira kũũrĩra…," our child, stop crying, stop crying, as she walked him around, slung on her shoulder, and rocked him. When that failed, she massaged him on the back as she repeated, "Thayũ mwana thayū," peace child peace. But the boy never quit crying.

Mother diagnosed him with a bellyache, wrapped him in a towel, and carried him in a cloth she tied over her shoulders like a sling. She invited me to accompany her to Mama Alan's house. It was my first time venturing outside the village gate.

It was almost dark when we arrived at the small mud-walled, grass-thatched shack, yards from Mũgono's thingira and a short distance from the hydrant where we drew water. Before Mother knocked on the wooden door or identified herself, the door creaked open. Mama Alan appeared, stooped over before she hung onto the door, and straightened herself.

"With those cries," she said, "I knew a sick child was on the way."

I stood beside Mother, transfixed. I had never seen such leathery skin or such a serious stoop.

She wore a couple of necklaces and several bangles, but no earrings through her holed, dangling earlobes.

When we entered, before Mama Alan returned to her seat in front of a slow-burning fire, she offered Mother a low bench, but none to me. I sat on the dirt floor by my mother, drew my knees in, rested my chin on top, hugged my legs, and watched.

The inside of the small house was warmer than I ever remembered ours, perhaps because we came from the cooler air outside.

Mother repeated her diagnosis of a bellyache.

"I'll take care of that," the village matriarch said.

She spread a gunnysack on the floor beside her, then fetched a small leather bag that contained knick-knacks. She felt inside and pulled out a small gourd, shook it, and placed it by her side.

"Let me have the child," she said as she rose and extended her arms.

Mother handed over Macharia, who kept up his screams, his voice hoarse by then. He displayed strained veins like tiny ropes down his temples and brow.

Mama Alan laid Macharia on the gunnysack and unwrapped the towel while he screamed and kicked. She took off his little shirt and handed it to Mother.

"Young lad," she said. "You'll get healed in no time. Where does it hurt? Here? There?" she asked Macharia as if she expected him to answer while she pressed spots on his tummy.

I wanted to say, "He cannot talk yet. He only makes ma-ma-ma sounds," but the words stuck within.

Mama Alan shook the small gourd again before she squeezed a dab of homemade mbarĩki (castor) oil onto her left palm, rubbed her palms, and spread them near the fire. When the oil warmed, she massaged Macharia's belly in a circular motion. After several rounds, she reached his back several times.

She replenished and warmed the oil twice.

By the time she finished work on his midriff, Macharia's screams had turned into intermittent whimpers.

She started another round from his head, shoulders, arms, and fingers, and on down to his thighs, legs, feet, and toes. Soon, Macharia's whimpers trailed off, and he fell asleep. Mama Alan wrapped the towel back around him and handed Mother her child.

*

Several months after Macharia's illness, at about age eight, I suffered a bellyache. Mother did not yet know how to give massages. Or perhaps she believed her touch could not heal as well as our masseuse. Instead, she took me to Mama Alan.

When we arrived, Mama Alan directed me to the gunnysack. Instead of taking off my dress, she rolled it up to my chest.

As she massaged my belly with the warm oil, smooth, calming sensations dulled the pain. My eyes struggled to stay open while my body relaxed into a state of euphoria where I longed to remain.

Against protests from every cell in my body, Mama Alan slowed her hands and stopped. She then ran cursory massages over my face and arms to remove oil from her hands.

I wished she could give me the same treatment as she gave Macharia, but she only gave full-body massages to little children.

Mother held my hand to steady me while we walked the one block home. When we arrived, I felt so heavy, calm, and safe that I skipped supper and went straight to bed.

34. Modern Conveniences

As our lives settled into routines that promised relief, Mother began to trust conveniences that would soon come with hidden costs.

Because the village was at a higher elevation, and it was difficult for me to walk back home, she had stopped taking me to her job to babysit for her since we moved to the village. Besides, she needed me to watch my younger siblings. From the beginning, she left Nyandia, four and a half, and Gĩthũi, two and a half, with me, with strict instructions not to loiter outside our courtyard. That posed no hardship for me; we were used to being confined in a courtyard at Kĩrĩma-inĩ.

She left our food in nyũmba for us to eat when we got hungry. We never waited for hunger pangs or sat down to eat. We rushed in between our play and scooped one fistful at a time. By midday, we had cleaned our plates. If, by chance, Mother had boiled maize and beans for our evening meal, we dipped in that, too. One day, she found only brown, watery dregs at the bottom of the clay pot. She had to hustle to find something else to cook for supper.

As babies, all of us children had accompanied Mother wherever she went, whether it was to her job, the garden, or to fetch firewood, and she suckled us until age two. So far, for the first year of his life, Macharia accompanied her.

Then, through her new village network of friends and acquaintances, Mother got lured into modern conveniences. To lighten her burden, she introduced Macharia to bottle-feeding. He breastfed at night or when she was home. Otherwise, he remained with me and fed from a bottle. When Mother returned home, she found him and the rest of us alive and well—at least most of the time.

If his food ran out, we chewed ours and fed it to him.

Macharia was the first child in my family to remain with older siblings before Mother weaned him from breastfeeding. He was also the first to feed on milk bottles and eat food from surrogate mouths. No wonder every few months he caught a disease that resisted Mother's *potions* or Mama Alan's oils and determined hands.

The disease baffled Mother because, according to her, my siblings and I had never caught colds or such illnesses before we moved to the village.

Whenever the mysterious disease struck, she fussed and said her child might die. The fear of one of us dying troubled her until we grew strong enough to withstand the attacks that bedeviled us in our first years in the village.

The first time the mystery disease attacked him, Macharia threw up from both ends of his little body. My mother rushed him to the clinic at Njeki's Shopping Center. Francis, the Luo medical assistant and the lone medic, considered it serious enough to refer her to Nakuru General Hospital, twenty miles away.

Since our area bus to Nakuru Town left only once a day, Mother waited until early the following morning. To sustain Macharia overnight, she now and then fed him a teaspoon of the water-like solution that Francis had given her.

She and Macharia spent a week at the Nakuru General Hospital on that first visit. They stayed a week each of the other two times he fell sick within that year.

I failed to understand Mother's concern and worry about death, something that sounded alien and beyond my imagination. Her absences were the ones that troubled me.

Every time she and Macharia returned home, he looked as healthy as one of those images featured on baby food cans. The entire household rejoiced. We took turns playing with him. Those of us who could handle his weight bounced him on our knees, and the not strong enough played peekaboo or mimicked his baby talk.

I recall looking at him and thinking I had never seen him so healthy. Perhaps the sickness and hospital treatment did him some good.

After each hospital visit, the medics prescribed a bottle of clear water and gave Mother a new baby bottle to replace the old one. They also issued her packets of powdered milk.

Did the healers know of a permanent solution, or were they merely lax? Whatever the case, they failed to appreciate that the modern conveniences they promoted to mothers did more harm in places like ours, where we had no clean water, indoor plumbing, or bathrooms.

For years, they remained ignorant that the free bottles they issued to mothers after hospital visits were the source of some of those diseases. And we, Macharia's siblings, impaired his health as well. He and we dropped his milk bottle anywhere in the house or courtyard, only to grab and stick it in his mouth when he cried.

If medics and European farmers could not figure out that rural African mothers needed to breastfeed—because they lived under different circumstances from European mothers—how could my mother and other village women know?

Even when the medics knew, they never disclosed what ailed a person. Perhaps they withheld what they knew, or believed peasants could not understand.

Mother never learned what Macharia suffered from, so she could take precautions. Decades later, I concluded that Macharia's illness was likely caused by contaminated water and feeding bottles.

But Macharia pulled away from the shadow of death. Between germ attacks, he grew older and eager to emulate the rest of us. He tossed his bottle aside and reached for a mug before he could hold it steady. From his insistence, Mother or any of us helped him with the mug until he got the hang of it.

Today, I wonder whether Macharia's illness strengthened Mother's resolve to be more vigilant in her activism for home remedies. She relied on them more and more.

35. Dentist

During Macharia's illness, none of us fell sick enough to see a doctor. Otherwise, sickness spread in quieter, more ordinary ways, starting with a runny nose, a loose tooth, or an occasional bellyache.

Soon, however, sickness preyed on us and settled into our household for several years. It attacked us one at a time, sometimes in twos, and finally, almost the entire household.

But Njerũ and Ndurumo, in their teens, never fell prey. Njerũ left for boarding school after one year in the village. But it made little sense that Ndurumo never became ill.

Throughout, I never associated sickness with Baba. He never fell sick—except once in my mid-teens that I know of. He caught a cold, groaned, and moaned lest the household forget his distress.

But now, for the rest of us, Mother included, ill-health never trailed far from us. To curb the maladies, my parents turned to home remedies and our healers. Well, maybe they were all along, but I noticed it between the ages of seven and eight.

They used our homestead as a makeshift mini-hospital, staffed with a self-styled doctor, nurse, and dentist, with a distinct division of labor.

Baba turned into a dentist.

When a villager suffered a toothache and visited the clinic, the prescription was always to pull out the tooth—for a fee, of course. But Baba offered the same service for free. Any villager who came to our courtyard to seek treatment became so grateful. Besides saving their money, they did not have to ask Kamunge for permission or miss a day of work.

When a patient endured a toothache all night long, as each claimed, they appeared in our courtyard early in the morning, before Baba left for work or on his weekend errands.

A patient, usually a man, shoulders hunched, head tilted, resting his achy jaw on his palm, shuffled into our courtyard with one or two men in tow.

The patient and his helpers headed to thingira, where operations took place.

The men made an impromptu appointment, and a brief consultation followed. Then Baba fetched his surgical gear—a sisal sack and a pair of pliers. He spread the sack on the living area floor, had the patient lie on their back, and had the supporting staff take their positions.

"Open your mouth," Baba said. "More! Open wide!"

He then went to work.

After several attempts, amidst sighs and grunts, Baba raised the pliers with the culprit lodged in its jaws for all to see. But when an aching tooth was at the back, it took some effort to coax it out. In one incident, a molar proved so stubborn that Baba nudged the handlers to be more vigilant. The two men restrained the patient—one pressed his legs down, the other his torso and midriff. Whenever the pain became excessive, the patient jerked this and that. When his reflexes failed to dislodge his captors, he increased the intensity of his guttural noises. Despite the dentist and his helpers' efforts, the molar remained lodged.

"The tooth seems welded into your gum," Baba said, withdrew his pliers, and the men released their hold. "I don't want to dislocate your jawbone."

"Do whatever you can," the patient said, as if his mouth were filled with mashed potatoes.

"I can't take a chance with your jaw."

"I didn't sleep a wink last night," the patient said, now seated hunched, his palm to his jaw. "It was like a drill digging into my jaw."

The men kicked suggestions around.

When they resumed, Baba held a screwdriver.

He pried the sides of the man's tooth. Satisfied it was time for the next tool, he laid the screwdriver aside and took the pliers.

By then, the man roared like one of Kamunge's bulls in heat.

I could barely stand hearing his ordeal. Fear grabbed me, and I wanted to abandon our vigil.

During Baba's efforts, the man's grunts had alerted us. We had taken positions at one side of thingira's doorway, huddled, and watched. Focused on his task, Baba had not noticed us. When he finally raised his pliers with the man's molar wedged between its jaws, we scampered away.

Witnessing what Baba's "patients" went through, no one in our family cared for his archaic dentistry. We kept our dental issues hidden from him.

*

I do not recall when my milk teeth started loosening, but it was definitely after we moved to the village. I felt a twinge whenever my tongue caught on one of my bottom front teeth. Soon, a sharp pain shot through the tooth whenever my tongue or food touched it.

My mind remained fresh with the two horrors that villagers endured under Baba's hand. I shuddered when I imagined a pair of pliers prying and pulling into my mouth. No way would I let his hands come close to my ailing tooth.

I kept my pain to myself; it was my secret.

In time, when food or tongue tripped the tooth, I twitched or made an ouch sound. As the frequency of the snappy, sharp pain increased, the burden of my secret became unbearable. I shared it with Machira in confidence.

But our family's comedian and reporter could not keep such a hot nugget to himself. That evening, he spread the breaking news throughout the entire household.

Mother asked me to let her test whether my tooth had loosened enough to come out. I shook my head and walked a few paces toward the door. I could not trust her with my tooth after watching her trick Machira once. With her forefinger and thumb in his mouth, she wiggled his tooth and, without warning, yanked it out. Machira yelped and whimpered.

"You didn't say you'll take it out!" he said.

"It was too loose," she told him. "If I left it, you would have twin teeth."

Her twin-teeth classic threat went beyond my imagination; I hadn't seen any twin teeth.

In my case, Mother left my tooth alone. She did not fool me—I knew her ploy; she was waiting for an opening. She could not help herself from adding a warning to my tooth worry.

"If it becomes too loose," she said, "it'll fall out, and you may swallow it with food."

I looked at her, wondering which was worse—pain or swallowing a tooth. But Machira, having gone through several tooth evolutions, settled the matter by sharing his wisdom.

The following day, my tooth remained a major topic in our courtyard. Machira, who had already gone goat herding, could not help me carry out the advice he had given me the previous night. It was now up to my younger siblings and me, and a couple of village children, to debate and decide on the best way to remove my tooth.

We dismissed Baba's dentistry outright.

There remained two options: first, let Mother pull out my tooth. Second, use Machira's method, which he either devised or picked up from village boys.

I had already turned Mother down. Machira's method had to be it. Tie one end of a string around my tooth and tether the other end to a post. Then snap my head back, and my tooth would snap the other way.

It distressed me to think about it.

After much anguish, I postponed my decision, content to wait until my tooth got looser.

Nobody said more about the matter, and I thought it was settled.

But Njerū, now fifteen, had come home from boarding school. After we moved to the village, he stayed one year—the specifics I recall little of—and then left. He seemed several rungs above us in shoes and clean clothes, and no manual labor for him. He hardly said a word to me unless he was addressing all of us. Now, seated on a stool by the granary, we had not paid attention to him as we went on and on about my tooth.

"Wanjirũ," he called me. I turned toward him, self-conscious that he had heard us.

"Huh," I said. That is the clearest image I recall of him before I turned eleven.

"Come closer," he said. "I'll help you assess how long the tooth will take to loosen."

"Assess" sounded reasonable, something I could handle.

Six feet from him, I opened my mouth and touched my ailing tooth and slightly wiggled it. "Look," I said, mumbling.

"How long do you think it'll take to loosen?" he asked.

I hesitated. How would I know that? I asked myself.

"I don't know," I said.

"Can I feel it?"

I inched closer to my brother, my plan to protect my tooth forgotten.

"Eeee," I said, my mouth open, my lower lip curled.

"Is this the one?" Njerũ asked as he touched each of my loose tooth's two neighbors.

I shook my head slightly.

The second his forefinger and thumb landed on my shaky tooth, he gripped and yanked it in one swoop.

"Ah!" I said in surprise. I then cried and cried. Not out of pain—it was a mere flash—but because of the tricky way he removed my tooth.

Subsequently, I never mentioned my wobbly teeth to anyone. When the time came for each tooth to depart my mouth, its roots loosened and finally rotted. My tongue periodically nudged the old crown outward while the new tooth inched and pushed upward. Finally, the poor rootless crown tipped over and dislodged.

Maybe my siblings used the same painless tactic because, after everyone's permanent teeth settled in, I noticed one of Ndurumo's old canines failed to tip over. It scooted slightly up his gum and latched onto the outside of its replacement. He ended up with fraternal twin canines on his upper gum.

To my credit—and to the rest of the family's—I never asked about or mentioned Ndurumo's twin teeth. And for consolation, Ndurumo remained well while the rest of us learned early on how pain or sniffles could arrive unannounced.

36. Treatments

Beyond teeth and sniffles, my parents managed illnesses in our household through routine treatments that they trusted and practiced.

Baba foraged for herbs and dug medicinal roots around the farm's woody areas when he went to set or check on his bee-hives. Occasionally, he returned home with a bundle of branches and roots, which he separated into herbs for general wellness and those for treatment. He then removed nodes, scraped loose bark, and cut the branches and roots into six-inch sticks and tied them into small bundles with sisal string. He gave the bundles to Mother to store in the granary.

Whenever Baba slaughtered a goat, depending on the herb he needed to use for whipping the soup, Mother boiled one bundle and strained the liquid. Or he grated the herbs into the soup with a blunt knife. Then he whipped the soup with kĩbĩrĩ or kĩbĩri—a wooden whip fitted with a dried goat's vertebra—until it foamed.

Some herbs made the soup flavorful, while others turned it bitter.

Herbal soups were supposed to strengthen the drinker's immune system. The bitterer the soup, according to my parents, the more effective it was. I hated the bitter ones and drank the rest only because they said so.

Baba was especially diligent about those soups after Mother gave birth. I overheard her and other women say that soups reset a new mother's bones and stimulate milk glands.

I noticed that Baba added certain herbs to the soups he drank or shared with other men. I never became curious about why.

I later learned that older men used, and still use, herbs from shrubs or the bark of trees like mũiri, an indigenous tree in Kenya. The herbs are supposed to guard against enlargement of the prostate gland or prostate cancer.

For health maintenance, men drank "tea" made from dried mũiri leaves once a day. If it was for treatment, they drank it straight twice or three times a day. Nowadays, some spike it with lemon and honey to tame the bitterness.

Mũringa was the other tree whose bark men dried and ground into powder. They drank a teaspoon, or an equivalent amount, of the bitter liquid a day for maintenance. A man doubled or tripled the intake if he fell sick. One could alternate Mũiri and Mũringa treatments.

*

While Baba used herbs for health maintenance and sickness prevention, Mother used them to treat her whole brood when more than one child sneezed and developed a runny nose.

She tied a variety of leafy branches into a bundle like a broom. Then boiled water in a big corrugated-iron basin and dipped the bunch into the boiling water, with the handle sticking out. She turned the leaves now and then; the fumes made her entire house smell like a hospital dispensary or pharmacy of days gone by.

When Mother determined the vapor was most potent, she placed the steaming basin at the center of the living area. She then arranged low benches around the basin and told us to sit.

Aware of Mother's occasional drill, Gĩthũi inched away from the group.

Unconcerned, Mother brought a blanket, sat on the highest stool, and threw it over the rest of us. She then ensured every gap was closed to prevent the steam from escaping. The inside turned pitch black and as hot as a sauna.

She told us to bend slightly toward the basin. Some complained about the heat; others asked whether we were well yet.

But our family's stubborn child insisted he was not sick and remained on the outside, his empty little bench on the inside. Amidst our chatter, we heard him walk about.

"Are you hot?" he asked at intervals. "Is it burning? You're taking too long. Are you done?"

I suppose Gĩthũi could not decide what bothered him more—freedom and loneliness or captivity and our company.

But he did not remain indecisive for long before curiosity and loneliness pushed him closer and closer to the igloo.

Mother took him by surprise when she raised the right side of her blanket, grabbed the six-year-old by the shoulder, and tucked him next to her as chickens do to their stray chicks.

"This vapor will travel through your nostrils and burn the cold," Mother told him.

"I don't have a cold to burn," Gĩthũi said before giving up his half-hearted struggle.

Mother turned the leaves every so often, and more swooshes of hot vapor assaulted our faces.

When she turned the leaves and they produced anemic heat-wave, she declared, "We are all done!" and threw off the blanket.

This brought excitement as we shrieked with bravado. "It was hot, and yet we braved it," we said. Even Gĩthũi had the nerve to exclaim twice, to ensure we heard him.

"Even me!" he said. "I did it!"

*

Mother believed her treatments failed only if she did not know what ailed a child.

But after a group's treatment, sometimes the well remained well, and the sick continued to swipe mucus off their noses with their backhands.

Mother had a ready explanation—the cold would have gotten worse without treatment, or that's why the rest of you didn't catch it.

But if the cold persisted, our family's *doctor*, nurse, and performer of a hundred other jobs—titled and untitled—had an answer for that, too.

"A mother with children," she said, "shouldn't knock on doors at midnight seeking treatment."

Her goal was to ensure we did not develop pneumonia or infect others. So she stocked her pharmacy in her bedroom and replenished it when it ran low.

When a cold became stubborn, she lathered the patient's chest with Vicks VapoRub and dabbed a little in each nostril.

In the absence of a mucus complaint, she felt the patient's brow with her backhand, then the chest with her palm to gauge how fast the heart thumped.

"I think it's pneumonia," she would announce. Based on her diagnosis, we had all caught pneumonia.

If Mother ruled out a stubborn cold and claimed one suffered from pneumonia, she augmented Vicks VapoRub with MB, a white, round tablet about four times the size of an aspirin, which she got from Francis, our trusted medical assistant, or bought in Nakuru Town.

She gave the dosage in a three-times-a-day regimen. For babies, she quartered the MB and split it into halves for an older child. She put the applicable dosage on a spoon and ground it into powder with the back of another spoon. She then added a little water, stirred, and fed it to the patient.

For a cough, she prescribed a tablespoon of golden cod liver oil once or twice a day, depending on its severity.

Whenever I endured a tablespoonful of the golden, smooth liquid, I washed my mouth afterward to lessen the taste and fishy smell. But occasional, teensy, smelly belches escaped and plagued my throat for the duration of the treatment.

In our house, the cod liver oil treatment rarely ended when symptoms did. Mother either forgot or might have believed persistence was protection and continued the regimen even after an individual stopped coughing.

37. Hybrid Treatments

In our household, illness no longer belonged to one system. Treatments blended—herbs, hands, clinics, and management—depending on urgency, distance, and belief.

There were no clinics in Solai when we moved to the village in mid-1953. If people fell sick, they took the only morning bus ride to Nakuru General Hospital, twenty miles away, along a rugged dirt road. It took an entire day to get treatment and catch the only return bus late afternoon.

Meanwhile, after a while, I learned that half a mile eastward across the Tindaress River was a sprawling colonial house set on about ten acres where Kamunge and his family lived. A two-acre orchard—where Njerũ and Ndurumo once helped themselves to oranges, and Njerũ paid dearly—snuggled in a lush shrubbery area that bordered Jumatatu Mountain range to the east and the river to the south.

On the northern side, about 50 to 100 yards from the colonial house, was a huge barn where Kamunge's family stored equipment and sacks of coffee, wheat, and maize awaiting shipment to the Kenya Farmers Association (KFA). In one corner, Memsahib, Kamunge's daughter-in-law, ran a free "clinic" to help their employees. She cleaned and bandaged wounds and treated minor ailments for the village children. However, my mother did not seek help from her because she believed she could treat us just as well. "I don't care for tiresome explanations," Mother used to say, meaning questions she did not intend to answer.

Still, when injury struck suddenly, belief gave way to necessity.

She had no choice at Kĩrĩma-inĩ when I was a toddler, and Nyandia was a baby. It was a Sunday, a market day, and Mother had awakened at the first rooster's crow at about 3:00 a.m. She packed what she needed for her trip, kindled the fire, cooked porridge, and kept it aside for the children.

Machira, still young enough to spend nights at nyũmba, heard the noise and left his bed. In the living area, he found Mother making tea. Now fully awake, he went and retrieved his leftover ugali from the corner where Mother had kept it for him the previous evening. He sat on one side of the fire pit across from Mother, who held Nyandia in her lap.

Mother cooled half a cup of tea for Machira and handed it to him. While he shifted to get comfortable, the small stool he sat on wobbled and gave way. He fell on his side, and his left arm ended up in the fire. Mother thrust Nyandia down and rushed to rescue Machira. During the rescue, his arm's skin peeled off.

The homestead erupted into restlessness when the commotion awoke the sleeping. Mother left Njerũ and Ndurumo to mind us, and, instead of going to the market, she and Baba walked the four miles to Kamunge's compound while she held the screaming, almost-five-year-old.

Fortunately, the arm burned only on the outside, and Machira could rest it on Mother's shoulder.

Kamunge's two German Shepherds announced my parents' arrival. Exhausted, Machira produced hoarse whimpers while veins bulged on his brow and temples.

Memsahib received details of her patient from one of her domestic workers during her morning tea. After she finished, she walked to her clinic and invited my parents in. As a numbing agent, she gave Machira a packet of sweets while she attended to his burns. Whenever the pain distracted him, he stopped munching and threw in a cry or two. Memsahib pushed his elbow to encourage him to stuff more sweets into his mouth to stop the pain. He believed her.

Over the years, whenever Machira talked about the burn incident, he told only the part about eating sweets. Even we, his family, never paid attention to or mentioned the leathery scar he carried on the length of his arm.

Other than Machira's incident, we never sustained injuries beyond scrapes and scratches, which we did not report; they healed without intervention, although Mother kept Dettol for such incidents.

For babies and young children with troublesome stomachs who cried but could not explain what ailed them, Mother became our masseuse instead of asking for free service too often. But she never reached Mama Alan's level of skill.

I recall her applying oil to my face and arms. I felt the roughness of her calloused hands, unlike Mama Alan's soft hands that got too old to work the land except for her tiny vegetable garden.

When massages failed to heal, Mother treated us instead of walking four miles to the clinic. By then, two years after we moved to the village, the Ministry of Health ran a two-room clinic at Njeki's Shopping Center.

Despite the distance and the charge, as soon as the clinic opened, villagers abandoned Memsahib's free services. They wanted little contact with Kamunge's family. Besides, they felt exposed as they walked through the large, gateless entrance and across half of the compound to the barn. And there were the two German shepherds to keep an eye on.

At the clinic, Francis tended to patients alone for years before the health department employed a part-time assistant for him. Several years later, the department hauled into the yard a small, two-room trailer on wheels for extra room for when they did vaccinations.

In a rare case of constipation, Mother kept a bottle of castor oil she bought at Patel's General Store. A half or a full teaspoonful got a patient's bowels moving.

Solai grew plenty of mbarĩki (Ricinus communis) plants with lots of seeds from which factories made castor oil. But nobody bothered our bountiful mbarĩki plants. However, as I grew older and took up activities outside our compound, I occasionally cracked a dry pod to admire the beautiful seeds, in black-and-white lines like zebras and auburn eyes at the tips, like precious stones. I suppose people could have chewed their seeds to get relief, but nobody did.

Although I do not recall using the castor oil treatment, my youngest sister, Wairimũ, wished she could when Mother used a never-before-seen treatment on her one Sunday afternoon.

Mother cooked us a late lunch when Wairimũ, at about four years old, sat tilted on one side, quiet and listless. She watched the rest of us chatter as we waited for our first major meal of the day since our morning porridge. She started whimpering and walking about, saying nothing.

"What's wrong with you?" Mother asked.

"My poop won't come out," Wairimũ said right there in front of everybody. Now that we all knew her secret, she whimpered, and in a minute her lips pouted and quivered.

Mother rushed to her "pharmacy" only to find she had overlooked replenishing her castor oil. With none of my brothers present to send to Patel's general store, I expected Mother to send someone to borrow the oil from our neighbor. But she had no time to waste. From her quickness, I could tell a novel idea had come to her.

Within a minute, she raised Wairimũ by her armpits, rushed her behind the granary, and laid her in a fetal position on the grass. She then rolled Wairimũ's dress to the waist, which left her little bare bottom sticking out.

Mother's index finger went to work. It pried marble-sized hard balls, some the size of pellets dropped by Baba's goats, from Wairimũ's backside while she let out a series of tiny sobs. She hushed as soon as the crude procedure ended.

After the treatment, Wairimũ disclosed that she had eaten heaps of kĩmande, maroonish seeds shaped like lentils that were high in fiber. Instead of chewing the seeds, swallowing the juice, and discarding the bulky fiber as we did, Wairimũ had swallowed everything.

She never touched those seeds again, even after we instructed her on the proper way to eat them.

Mother treated everything—eyes, stomachs, breathing, and more.

When my baby sister's or brother's eyes got sick and swelled, Mother let the baby finish breastfeeding. She then patted the baby's eyelids, pointed her nipple, and squeezed drops of milk into both eyes. In days, the sickly eyes cleared. She did the same to my baby brother's penises.

We asked her why.

"It'll help it open so he can pee properly."

She had a cure for labored breathing, too. When an infant had clogged nostrils and struggled to breathe, Mother sucked the snot out of its nose and spat it out. Yuck!

Although I said nothing the two times Machira paraded around without a shirt on, I thought my parents' treatment had gone too far. I noticed four razor-keloid scars about an inch long on his left rib cage.

I don't know whether anyone else saw it, but no one spoke or mentioned it. I suspect Mother or Baba bled him after he developed high fever or pneumonia, Mother's default ailment.

With us getting sick one at a time, Mother looked like a wizard. She prescribed treatment or took a patient to a doctor, and within a week—Poof!—the disease disappeared.

But even when illness vanished, Mother never relaxed; fear lingered longer than symptoms. She occasionally said, "Let me see your eyes," or when we played in the courtyard, she would ask, "Is someone coughing out there?" Just as well, because she noticed the first signs when the Big Two hit back-to-back.

38. Predatory Viruses

We were used to health hazards like scrapes, stomachaches, and sniffles attacking us, one child at a time. Mother could manage those. But it turned out to be a burden for her when gĩthũkũ (measles) swept through our household and cast its spell on our collective.

It snuck onto one of us; nobody learned who. Then spread until it affected all six of us children. Mother had to stay home to nurse her patients.

When we looked at her with sad eyes that implied, "Do something," as if she read our minds, she said, "I won't take you to the hospital; doctors don't treat measles."

Even Francis? Her favorite medical officer? I asked myself. I thought he could cure any disease.

After Mother's dim announcement, she remained the only person we could count on. We lived and thrived based on her knowledge and actions—a simple fact of childhood.

Mother fussed and stressed not only because we refused to eat but also because she lacked a magic cure. "A child needs to eat something to fight the disease," she said, and insisted we eat.

At one point, she brought little pieces of scrambled eggs to my mouth. I remember thinking, I'm not a baby while I shook my head. She coaxed me to take just one bite. I tightened my lips and turned sideways. The mere smell caused my diaphragm and throat to convulse.

Was Ngai punishing me because of my greed? I wondered. I once wished I could fall sick so Mother could feed me eggs. And now I can't stand their sight or smell?

Besides chicken, which we considered a special meal because we rarely ate it and, when we did, given our large family, one piece each was not enough to satisfy our palates, eggs were the other delicacy that fell into that category. My siblings and I hardly ate them.

I cannot think of a reason we never ate eggs when we lived at Kĩrĩma-inĩ; Baba had plenty of chickens. But now in the village, he owned about half that number or fewer. They could not lay enough eggs to hatch and leave some for the family. And even if they could, because eggs were easier to sell, Mother would have sold them as she did with the extras and bought what she, like other mothers, considered necessities, like sugar and cooking oil.

Mother spared eggs only when we fell sick. But we frowned at that type of "treatment."

If she could not feed us to starve the measles, however, she turned to the next alternative to help us heal faster. She washed us with Baba's homemade beer and gave us a sip after every wash. The color had a clear yellow tinge, and the taste was unexpectedly milder than the bitter soups Baba whipped up.

Measles affected all of us the same way, but, unlike my siblings, my right eye remained shut for weeks, or for as long as measles ravaged our bodies. Mother worried I might become mono-eyed. But unlike my baby siblings, she did not prescribe breast milk drops for my eye. Instead, she parted both eyelids every day and checked. Like other rural mothers, she sometimes spat on her finger and brushed boogers off my eye, which I detested, especially now that I was almost nine, albeit a tiny nine.

After I healed, she checked my right eye and announced it had a njereri (a floater). I did not ask her what that meant; after all, I saw as well as before.

Years later, during a routine eye exam, an optometrist found a scar on the retina of my right eye and said I did not see as clearly with that eye as with my left. For decades afterward, I never noticed the difference unless I shut my left eye. Then one day, I saw a faint squint that wasn't in my earlier photos. Only then did I realize—almost by accident—that my right eye was slightly smaller than the left, something I had been born with but had never noticed.

*

Measles retreated gradually, the same way it had sneaked up on us. Mother glowed when she saw us go outdoors. "A child who doesn't play is sick," she used to say.

We soon engaged in our activities, and she declared us cured.

Before we settled into our health, however, another malady snuck up on us. While we sat around the fire, Mother looked at Machira and said, "It seems measles left your body weak." We all turned toward him. His uncovered thighs and arms looked unusually ashy, with trails of nail scratches.

In two days, Nyandia and I started itching and scratching, and Gĩthũi soon joined us.

Mother said we suffered from mũthandũkũ (chickenpox).

Soon, the itching became so severe that our scratches left ashy streaks all over our skin like Machira's. Tiny pimples started to sprout throughout our bodies, even in our mouths. They grew larger by the day, and some developed into big bumps.

Mother said not to scratch, no matter how much our skins begged.

"If you scratch," she said, "you'll have scars for the rest of your life."

The rest of my life meant nothing to me, but I made efforts to follow her wishes. Sometimes my resolve broke, and I sneaked satisfying scratches behind her back. I suppose she expected it because she monitored us.

Whenever she saw any of us wince and wiggle, she called out. "No scratching! Don't you scratch!"

Chickenpox, however, did not devastate us as much as the measles. We could still move about in the courtyard and out of Mother's sight. It became harder and harder for her to keep an eye on us, although her voice echoed within me.

When an area itched excessively, I tightened my body. If I failed to get relief, I rubbed my palm over my dress until the critical itchy wave passed.

Mother restarted her beer regimen. According to her, the disease attacked from the inside, and the beer therapy would stimulate pimples to the surface. The more bumps sprouted, the faster we would heal, she said.

The back-to-back sicknesses so overwhelmed Mother that she stopped or forgot to evoke, "This disease will kill my children," that she indulged in back in the damp hovels at Kabati and during the measles attack.

In a week, the bumps filled with fluid. Even without scratching, some bumps ruptured when we sat, rubbed against clothes, or turned in bed. They left open sores that dried into scabs. When they healed, they left scars like any other wound. But the bumps that remained intact dried out like aged skin and finally flaked off.

I'm not sure how long chickenpox dotted our bodies—days or weeks blurred together. But when we started playing—a sign we had healed well enough—our bodies displayed spots like those of a cheetah. Gĩthũi's spots ended up the biggest, some the size of a dime or a cent. Mother said he would carry scars for the rest of his life. But as his body filled out, the spots disappeared.

That was the last time my family fell ill together. Afterward, sickness came singly, never again as a sweep.

39. Lethal Bite

Family illness may have disrupted Mother's work schedule, but our household's rhythm remained unchanged. She took care of the sick and her other chores despite the stress and worry she shouldered.

After the illnesses passed, we assumed life would simply continue. She and Baba had even gotten together between Macharia's hospital trips, as we soon learned.

When Macharia turned two, and I eight, Wawerũ came along—another boy for me to babysit.

But, as good mothers do, mine had already trained me to be a well-rounded, obedient native daughter. After months of taking Wawerũ to her job, she put him on a bottle and left him with me as she had done with Macharia.

Taking care of a baby all day long posed no strain for me. Even if it did, it failed to register. I knew no other way. It was normal, and "poor-me" never crossed my mind. At nine years old, I played house with other children, my baby brother strapped to my back. We picked weeds to imitate coffee cherry pickers at the scrubby bushes that grew between our granary and my parents' garden, which they had established next to the towering fence.

The only times I asked another child or Nyandia to help me hold or watch Wawerū were when it was my turn to play hop-scotch or jump rope.

Like Macharia, when Wawerū cried when his food ran out, we chewed our food for him. But if milk ran out, or before Mother cooked something for him when she returned, whoever held him shushed him by sticking a tongue or a lower lip into his mouth.

That did not fool him. He fussed until he got what he wanted.

*

Mother seemed indestructible to me; I had never seen her sick. But things changed after she nursed us back to health, which revealed—something we had taken for granted before—how crucial she was to our lives.

Her journey into sickness began with a trip to the garden to cultivate and pick vegetables. That evening, while we sat around the fire in thingira, where she occasionally cooked to save on firewood, she said something bit her ankle. "I was pulling weeds under dense bean plants," she said, "when I felt a sharp prick."

"What was it?" Gĩthũi asked, young enough to butt into adults' conversation and in Baba's presence.

"I don't know."

"You didn't check?" Baba asked.

"I had to let the pain pass first," she said. "But when I brushed aside the dense plants, I saw nothing."

"There are lots of insects this time of year," Baba said. "Could it have been a wasp?"

"My mind tells me it could've been a snake," she said softly as if she hoped it wasn't.

"It's hard to tell," Baba said.

"It broke the skin."

Except for Gĩthũi, none of us children said anything.

With her evening chores and us children waiting for food, Mother ignored her leg until after supper. By then, her leg had swollen, but it did not seem bad enough to alarm my parents. They would decide in the morning if the leg got worse, they said.

When I awoke, Mother sat in her usual spot by the fire pit in nyũmba, making morning tea, her fat leg outstretched over a low bench. The leg had grown bigger and looked shiny, like a puffed sausage. She remained seated and sent us to fetch whatever she needed to make breakfast.

We eyed her, confused and subdued.

Late in the afternoon, when Baba returned from work, Mother labored to breathe and spoke with difficulty.

I am unsure whether Baba asked Kamunge for transportation on the tractor-drawn wagon, but my father lamented that Mother was too sick to wait for the bus in the morning. He sent for Francis.

Still in his white coat, clutching a black doctor's bag, Francis walked the four miles from the clinic to our homestead. When he arrived, our entire family relaxed. Mother trusted and believed in his diagnosis and treatment as a follower would a cult leader. She also liked that she could speak with him in Kiswahili, unlike at the big hospital, where she relied on nurses to translate English for her.

"You can't be sure 'sisters' always tell you what the doctor says," she once told her friend when they talked about the cons of the big hospital.

Francis gave Mother a shot. He said not to bother going to Nakuru General Hospital because they used the same antivenom.

Mother remained bedridden for about a week, and Ndurumo, then fifteen, gave her a washcloth bath twice. He also did housework and cooked for us.

My siblings and I never saw our mother during that period. Our only contact with her was hearing her voice when she grunted, asked for help, or gave instructions to Ndurumo.

Then, one mid-morning, Mother grew tired of staying in bed and asked Ndurumo to help her go outdoors for some sun. Somehow, Ndurumo got her off the bed.

When my younger siblings and I played in the courtyard, I turned toward the porch when I heard Mother's voice. She lay on the ground, leaning on her elbow, with Ndurumo standing beside her. Too heavy for him to lift, he hesitated, unsure of what to do.

"Leaning against the granary boards would be better," Mother said with difficulty.

"That's too far," Ndurumo said.

"I'll try to get there."

Mother crawled sideways on dirt, an inch at a time, dragging her half-covered, log-sized leg, punctuating every move with a sigh or a grunt. Ndurumo remained beside her, taking an occasional small step.

The puffed leg looked so shiny as if it would sizzle and burst. She took breaks in between, leaned on Ndurumo, and then resumed her crawl.

Halfway to the granary, she tried several times to reach out, plant fingers on the ground, and push herself forward. But she did not move an inch. Her body had exhausted itself. Finally, she gave up. "Getting to the granary will take me all day," she said, panting.

Then she struggled to sit up. She could not do that either. Her body looked lopsided. Besides, the humongous leg weighed too much for her to handle.

She planted her elbow on the ground and asked Ndurumo to get her a chair to lean on.

While Mother struggled to keep her head up, my younger siblings and I remained transfixed, watching from afar, standing between the goats' cottage and the boys' thingira.

The huge leg scared me. I had not seen a snake by then, but from my parents' description, I feared a snake might have slithered into Mother's leg. And worse, I resigned myself to having a helpless mother who could no longer walk.

She craned her neck and looked at our miserable group.

"Ûũi, Mwathani," (Ohh, Lord), she said softly. "My own children are afraid of me."

We said nothing. We just stood there, expressionless, our sober eyes on her.

Ndurumo brought a folding wooden chair. When he unfolded it, Mother raised her torso and barely rested her elbow on the chair as he pushed it little by little toward her. With her torso raised, she basked in the sun.

I doubt she got comfortable because she tried to shift several times and failed each time. Her face was flushed and strained from the tropical sun and the effort.

She stayed about ten minutes, if that, before she asked Ndu-rumo to help her crawl back indoors.

As Mother struggled to manage our household through Ndurumo, no one mentioned the hospital again. Francis had already taken care of it, and that was that.

Gradually, she improved to a point where she could crawl outdoors without Ndurumo having to keep guard.

Perhaps confident about Mother's recovery, Baba finally spoke up; he told us about his dance with disability.

*

One late afternoon in Kĩrĩma-inĩ, before I was born, Baba walked from the courtyard to his thingira. When he reached the threshold, he heard rustling, likely after something he carried touched the rafters.

The instant he looked up, a spray of liquid hit right into his eyes. He cried out in pain and groped for the entrance, already sure what had attacked him. When someone answered his call, the snake, which I now guess was a cobra, had slithered away.

Baba sent Waigwa, my half-brother, to report to Kamunge and get some medicine. He returned with a small bottle of eyedrops.

Despite Baba constantly applying antivenom drops, his eyes remained swollen shut. After two weeks without improvement, he became desperate and began to lament. "How will I earn a living as a blind man?" he asked himself. "Kamunge will eject me from the farm. Where will my family go?"

He lived with the likelihood of homelessness for an entire month. Fortunately, he didn't share his fears with the family.

Then, slowly, the swelling subsided, and his sight gradually returned.

"Don't worry about your mother," he now said. "She'll heal just like I did."

It eased my mind when Baba said those words; things always turned out as he said they would. It meant I would not get stuck with a mother who moved about on her knees.

As Mother's leg healed, the swelling subsided to where she could hobble and support herself by holding onto a wall or doorway, and rest without putting weight on her leg. Baba made her a wooden crutch to ease her hobble.

Meanwhile, her leg skin, from her hip to her foot, began to peel like snakes shed their skins. By the end of the second month, her leg had brand-new skin like a newborn's.

Life resumed, but none of us forgot how close it had come to stopping or being completely altered.

40. The Surrogate Mother

After Mother healed from the snakebite, I treated her illness as incidental and put it out of my mind.

But within that year, she complained of throbbing pain on one side of her rib cage. She winced if she moved and could not sleep on that side. Even her breathing became increasingly labored.

Just like before, Ndurumo picked up cooking, which confirmed Mother's serious condition.

For the first time, Kamunge donated his rickety tractor-drawn flatbed wagon to take her to the bus stop. Baba never mentioned the agony she must have endured on Kamunge's rocky road, the long bus ride, or the walk to the hospital.

Late that afternoon, my heart sank when Baba entered the courtyard alone. "The doctor said your mother needs to remain in the hospital," he said.

Did the doctor say how long? I wondered. I hungered for more details. But Baba said nothing else.

My mother's ill health worried me, and I hated how it had disrupted our household's routine and cadence. I hated her absence the most, especially that hospital admission. In her previous absences, she had taken the baby with her. But she couldn't this time. I had to mind Waweru day and night as a mother would.

Rumors reached me that a woman said perhaps Mother suffered from residual snake venom. I did not dwell on it. Women always talked and sometimes made unfounded claims. Although I perked my ears to catch their gossip whenever I went to the hydrant, the women's assertions meant little unless my mother concurred.

Baba proved helpless and of no help to us, yet again. Unless he asked a question or wanted one of us to fetch him an item, he did not deal with us in Mother's absence. And never brewed or drank beer.

Whenever he returned home from work or the garden, he checked on the goats. After he saw them safely in their cottage, he did little else besides confine himself in thingira.

If someone dropped by our homestead, Baba said, "The children's mother is away," without saying where she had gone unless asked.

A generous person to a fault, I now believe he wanted them to know he could not offer them tea or food.

At suppertime, when Ndurumo or someone else took him food, he asked, "Have the children eaten?"

That was the extent of Baba's involvement with housekeeping.

*

As if Mother's sickness did not weigh on me enough, my youngest brother, Waweru, a toddler shy of two years old, whom I was now in charge of, fell sick. He refused to eat or drink anything during the day. As Mother did, I tested him by laying the back of my hand on his brow. Next, I put my palm on the left side of his chest. Based on his brow temperature and heart's rapid thumps, I concluded he suffered from a serious illness. I guessed pneumonia, but I did not say it.

"Wawerũ is sick," I told Baba when he returned from work. "He threw up when I fed him, and his heart beat fast."

Baba came close to where I held Wawerũ in my lap, his head on my chest. After observing him, Baba left and returned about an hour later.

The following morning, he did not leave for work. Instead, he did something I never expected him to do. He took Wawerũ to Nakuru General Hospital. But not by himself. He needed someone to carry the baby. At nine years old, and the firstborn daughter of his second family, I went with him.

After the hospital check-up, the doctor announced Wawerũ was too sick to return home. He admitted both him and me so that I could mind him. I accepted my fate without rancor. To my relief, the nurse lifted Wawerũ from my lap and placed him on her shoulder, where he rested his head.

Free of child, my body relaxed and became lighter. I longed for a long stretch, but I stifled it because of the adults around me.

"Let's go," the nurse told me.

I rose from the chair and tightened my body to steady myself. By then, Wawerũ had been strapped to my body for twenty-one miles, three of which I had walked with him on my back.

As we walked through the corridor, I wondered what it would be like to sleep away from home. Although I felt iffy about the unknown, I did not feel fearful, abandoned, or sad. Before my father left, he assured me the hospital people would take care of my brother and me. I did what my parents told me without question. Besides, the nurse and, as it turned out, most of the people who worked in that ward spoke in Gĩkũyũ.

I reminded myself that the doctor had admitted me to act as a surrogate mother to my little brother, which, in my mind, meant I needed to represent my parents well.

Besides, Mother—my main anchor in life—languished in one of the hospital wards. Perhaps someone would take me where they kept her, a thought crossed my mind.

At the end of the corridor, we left that building and entered a children's ward lined with cots on both sides, with a shiny, smooth concrete floor and windows on both lengths of the building.

Mothers sat beside the cots or cradled children in their laps. I only realized later that those mothers spent their nights there, leaning against the cold walls. As we passed, older children, whose mothers could not stay with them, turned to us with sunken, subdued eyes.

Halfway inside the ward, the nurse deposited Waweru into a baby cot that he and I would share during our hospital stay. The sides of the cot reached to my armpits, much lower than the woven bed I shared with my sister Nyandia, which was so high it had an entrance like a treehouse.

I could climb in and out of our hospital bed without difficulty. But the bed held Waweru captive until his health improved. From then on, whenever he awoke, he stood, gripped the railing that reached to his chest, and waited for a nurse without a peep. A quiet child, he never tried to get out. We both waited—he inside the cot, I on the outside leaning against its railing. I would have lifted him out, but the railing was too high for me. Besides, my arms were not strong enough to bear his weight.

Waiting became part of our lives there.

41. The Cold-Water Hose

With a different routine and sharing a bed with Wawerũ, who wore no diapers, hospital life quickly taught me how little control I had.

The two of us awoke every morning with our gowns drenched in his urine. Most times, a nurse wiped him with a damp washcloth. She then gave me a gown and asked me to change while she dressed him.

With no one to remind me to pee before my bedtime, I had an accident on two nights. I dreamed I was going to the toilet. When I awoke, I realized I had instead added to the drench that guaranteed our trip to the cold shower room. But that was just the beginning.

Every morning, two nurses—patients called them "sisters"—came in. They wore light blue or green uniforms with white caps. One pushed a big bin, and the other dragged a smaller cart with clean bedding and tie-back gowns.

I saw this only when the nurses reached our cot, and one of them shook me awake. Unlike at home, where my body's circadian rhythm knew when to wake up, I would have slept through the stench and breakfast.

When the nurse woke me, I got out and stood by our bed. The minute my soles hit the concrete floor, the shock jolted me. An icy chill ran up my legs, and my toes rose. The bin nurse lifted Wawerũ and deposited him beside me. He immediately bunched his toes. He looked disoriented, his little gown crumpled and barely covering his front and bottom.

The nurse then stripped off the wet sheets, threw them into the big bin like discards, and wheeled it to the next cot.

The second nurse remained behind to tidy up and take us to the shower for our daily wipes. Before she took us, we waited while she wiped the thick, waterproof tarp-like green pad that protected our mattress, then made the bed with fresh sheets.

At home, we did not bother with cleaning as the nurses did. With dirt floors, urine got absorbed, and its smell got mixed with the chickens' and goats' smells. We scooped a baby's poop with velvety leaves called maigoya.

I now wonder how Mother stayed clean while sharing her bed with a little one. But when she weaned each of us—like a product on a conveyor belt—we moved from her bed to ours. Afterward, the last two children distracted her. From then on, the rest of us urinated in our beds without fuss. It was almost dry by the next bedtime.

This went on until the stench alerted Mother to her children sleeping in filth. She rounded us up on a Saturday and told us to take our bedding outside. We dried them spread over the stick fence or on the grass behind the granary. Used to hanging clothes on the fence at Kĩrĩma-inĩ, I suppose nobody thought of putting up a clothesline.

Once in a long while, Mother washed the rags that passed for our bedding.

*

On one occasion at the hospital, Wawerũ outdid himself. I woke up, and while rubbing my eyes to orient myself, the stench assaulted my nostrils. I turned my head down. The odor and sight of our two bodies made me cringe.

Urine and feces covered us from the rumpled gowns down to our feet. It embarrassed me that Wawerũ's behavior exposed our family to the clean, well-dressed hospital people.

Although I hadn't witnessed that much filth at home before, I realized my family didn't measure up, and that I needed to keep that part of our lives private.

"Oh! These children!" the nurse said the minute she laid eyes on our filthy bodies.

My insides squirmed as she tightened her face, narrowed her eyes, and shook her head slowly, making soft noises in her throat. She then stretched her arms and lifted Wawerũ from his armpits. His soiled bottom and legs dangled as she hustled him, her body bent forward toward the shower room.

"Come!" she said to me.

Confused, Wawerũ let out muffled whimpers.

Instead of washing him in a plastic basin half-filled with cold water as the nurse had done before, or letting me wash myself as I always did, the nurse deposited him at the center of the shower room.

"Stand by your brother!" she ordered me.

I hesitated, then did as I was told, confused, just like Wawerũ, who raised his hands toward me. In seconds, I realized what the nurse was about to do.

From a distance, slightly bent so the filthy water would not spray her, she pointed the hose at us and opened the spigot. The first splash almost knocked Wawerũ down and made me sway. The cold water had a bite I had never experienced before. At home, Mother would have claimed we would catch pneumonia. We never washed with cold water.

Wawerũ cried until his throat turned hoarse. He grabbed my arm and clung to my side to avoid the spray and steady himself on the slippery floor. Because he couldn't maintain his grip, I held him tight by the shoulder. I released him when the spray stopped, and he could stand without the danger of falling.

He stood with his little fists clenched. His body trembled from head to his bunched toes while his front teeth—the only ones he had—gritted as his lips vibrated and produced a humming sound.

I shivered too, but held tight, willing the ordeal to end.

The nurse kept up the occasional click of her tongue until she dried us. She then thrust a gown toward me while she dressed Wawerũ.

I thought we deserved it. This was the only time I remember thinking that way.

After all, I reasoned, *she is not our mother.*

Fortunately, although there was no warm fire like at home, a warm breakfast awaited us. They usually fed us porridge with milk or cocoa milk and bread with lots of butter.

We ate quietly.

42. Hospital Nuances

After one week at the hospital, I became aware of who did what work, who spoke, who listened, and who made decisions.

Each morning, a male medic stopped by our cot and read the notes on the clipboard hanging on the wall. He gave Wawerŭ medicine and noted it on the clipboard.

Twice during our stay, a group of white doctors, including one who looked Indian, in white coats came and held a discussion right there by the cot. The oldest, who made rounds in the mornings, checked Wawerŭ and discussed his findings with the rest before moving on to the next patient. They stayed longer at some cots than at others, especially at the older children's cots. Besides getting information from the nurses, they never spoke to the children.

A white woman, who accompanied the group, visited the ward at random. She wore a white dress, a belt snug on her midriff, white shoes, and a sturdier white cap with colored stripes, unlike the plain ones the other nurses wore. She talked to the nurses, stopped at a patient's cot, or gave instructions.

Patients called her "Big Sister."

Whenever Big Sister entered the ward, nurses focused on their jobs without speaking to colleagues, and if they did, they kept their voices low. Big Sister acted in charge, giving instructions and asking questions.

One morning, she came with the older white doctor (the term "doctor" meant male back then), and the two went from bed to bed, checking on patients. They reached where Waweru and I stood by our cot, waiting for our nurse to finish making our bed and attend to us.

While the doctor checked the clipboard, Big Sister told our nurse to return Waweru to the cot. The doctor then did his usual routine—listened to Waweru's chest and back with a stethoscope and checked his eyes.

Afterward, the two—the doctor and Big Sister—remained by our cot while they talked in a language I had never heard when I arrived at the hospital, but by then I had learned it was English, white people's language.

When the two turned their backs and moved a distance from us, a nurse close by snapped her chin toward them. "What diseases are they saying she will catch?" the nurse said softly in Kiswahili. "There are diseases right here."

"If I were in charge," our nurse said, "I'd let these children visit their mother."

I had noticed that the nurses spoke Gĩkũyũ among themselves and English with senior personnel. They used Kiswahili when they wanted to be understood or to conceal something from non-Kiswahili speakers.

As a nine-year-old Gĩkũyũ girl in 1956, I doubt the nurses expected me to speak or understand Kiswahili. But I did, although I don't recall when I learned the language, and even then,

I didn't realize I could speak two languages. I must have learned it when my family moved to the village and encountered people who were non-Gĩkũyũ. Tugen men dropped by our household to consult Baba about work, and I probably picked up the language during those interactions.

By then, we had already lived in the village for three years.

I felt kindly toward the two nurses because I knew if they had the power, they would let me visit my mother. Did she know Wawerũ and I were in one of the wards? I wondered.

Based on the work the doctor and Big Sister did, and how timidly the others behaved around them, I concluded they held the power. But they seemed so far removed from me; I expected no special consideration from them.

Even if they did not let me visit my mother, I felt grateful to the hospital people who cleaned, made our bed, fed us, and treated Wawerũ.

I even excused the silly hospital gown they issued me—an imitation dress. The wide neckline slid down my upper arm and exposed my right shoulder. I let it hang until it irritated me long enough. To keep the neckline in place, I flipped up the crook of my elbow occasionally, like one suffering from a shoulder tic.

Because I had no chores and did not carry or feed Wawerũ, except sit with him when he became well enough to join me outside, it felt, briefly, like a vacation of sorts for me.

I frolicked and skipped around the enclosed yard during the day. Because the other children were too sick to play, however, I never got into any mind- or body-stimulating activities.

But I enjoyed gawking, eavesdropping, and listening to mothers talk about their families and their sick children. They said their husbands visited them on Sundays when they were off work.

Occasionally, amid my play, I exchanged glances or a few words with children around my age who became fit enough to venture outside to get some sun but not strong enough to play. Between talking to the children, mealtimes, and listening to grownups, I never felt lonely. And because most, if not all, mothers spoke in Gĩkũyũ, like in my village, and my mother was in one of the hospital wards, I never missed home either.

Most late afternoons, though, I looked at the women, and a sharp whiff of loneliness stabbed me, and I longed to see my mother. I then stopped whatever I was doing, looked around the buildings, and wished I knew which ward they treated her in. I could then sneak in for a minute and visit her.

I briefly mulled over the thought before I realized such a daring venture went beyond my capabilities; I could get lost. Besides, sneaking away with adults all around me felt so daunting. I doubted they would let me loiter around the wards.

Baba came to check on us the following week. A nurse must have told me because I do not recall seeing him.

I can only surmise he did not know the ward they put us in, and he had to wait in the hospital's main waiting area. When he finally got someone to direct him, he found Wawerũ asleep, and me outside. A nurse gave him an update, and then he rushed to visit Mother before the visiting hour ended.

Before Baba returned a second time, however, the doctor and the Big Sister came to our cot again. The doctor checked Wawerũ while he and the Big Sister talked back and forth. Our regular nurse stood aside and waited. As usual, the doctor wrote on the clipboard.

After they finished, the Big Sister talked to our nurse in English before she and the doctor proceeded to the next cot.

"The doctor said your brother has healed," our nurse told me in Gĩkũyũ. "Your parents can take you home."

I indulged in a moment of joy before reality set in.

My mind churned.

Does she mean we leave today? I wondered.

Yes, we could leave. I had heard Mother and other women say buses never charged a child my age or younger unless she occupied a seat.

But could I stand and hang onto a seat frame with Wawerũ on my back when the bus reached the bumpy dirt road?

Perhaps a woman will offer to hold Wawerũ, or the conductor will give me a free seat.

But would he let me travel alone with a toddler?

If he does, and the bus drops us at the Solai Road bus stop, I can walk the two miles home.

But I do not know my way to the bus stop in town, I reminded myself. Perhaps Big Sister will let a nurse take us.

I reached a dead end, plagued by childhood dependence. My thoughts and wishes led nowhere and seemed useless. Somehow, I never expected the hospital to release us without Baba.

And I now doubt the personnel knew the location of Kamunge's farm, where they could find my father. If they recorded patients' "addresses" at all, they used the names of the farms where those patients worked.

Although it was beyond my capacity to think that way, I did not know the real name of my father's employer or the farm's name—people called the farm gwa-Kamunge (Kamunge's place). I accepted with dismay that my brother and I would remain wards of the hospital, at least for a time.

But I should not have worried myself. Although the medics stopped Wawerũ's medical treatment, the nurses treated us the same as before. They cleaned after us; we slept, ate, waited for Baba, and I thought about my mother.

Waiting had become familiar but more unsettling.

43. Instant Relief

Good food and treatment, and no chores, did nothing to dull my craving to return home, a need that heightened when someone reminded me.

"I thought the doctor discharged these children," a nurse said while she stood by our cot.

I shot her a look while my little chest contracted.

"We are waiting for someone to come for them," our nurse said.

Each day, I felt embarrassed, as if my brother and I were intruders.

A woman seated outside among a group of mothers once asked me, "When are your parents coming to get you?"

"Baba?" I asked.

The woman dipped her head and gave me a withering look as if to say, "Mind your manners."

"I don't know," I said.

"Where is your mother?"

"In the hospital."

The women exchanged knowing glances and comments about "the poor children." None of them asked me about going home again.

But I kept vigil. I stood in the side yard, where patients (and mothers) who could go outdoors spent most of their daytime hours. Occasionally, I looked over the short, shrubby fence at each man who walked by wearing a hat and coat, hoping it would be my father.

I could see an average man only from the chest up, but I was sure I would recognize Baba if he appeared.

I did this routine for days—maybe a week—and wondered whether Baba had become too busy and forgotten us. Then Wawerũ and I would turn wards of the hospital.

I had heard my mother and women familiar with hospital culture say that some families dumped their incurables and never returned.

I did not think Baba would abandon us; we were not incurables. Perhaps he just got too busy. I overlooked that he could only come on a Sunday, his day off.

One day, I saw a man amble toward the hospital buildings from a distance. I squinted and looked as usual. The man looked familiar. I squinted again in case my eyes tricked me. As he got closer and closer, I saw it was really my father.

Great relief rose within me. It turned into excitement. I balled my fists, put them next to my cheeks, and watched until Baba disappeared inside. Emotions tumbled within me. But besides waiting for the nurses, I wondered what to do next. I moved about, stayed in a place for a while, and moved again. To unsettle me even more, the two nurses who had cared for us and knew our plight were off duty that weekend.

I remained in limbo for a long, long time—perhaps half an hour. The waiting ravaged my insides.

Then a nurse came.

"Your father is here to get you," she said.

I said nothing. I did not know what to say.

The nurse carried Wawerũ astride her hip, and I followed.

She had already hung our miserable clothes—a dress, a shirt, and ngoi—on the cot's railing. After we changed into our clothes, she secured Wawerũ to my back and led the way.

We found Baba in the waiting room.

"Wĩmwega?" (How are you?), he said.

"Ndĩmwega" (I am well), I said.

"How is your brother?" He bent over to look at Wawerũ.

"He got well."

On our way to catch the late afternoon Solai bus, Baba said, "Your mother is already at home."

"Is she healed?"

"Yes, she's healed."

The news made me so happy that I could not wait to get home. From that minute, I retained no single memory of our trip home.

*

Mother rushed out of nyũmba when she heard Baba's voice.

"My children are home!" she said when she saw us. She unloaded Wawerũ from my back and placed him astride her hip.

I experienced instant relief that I still recall. Similar to our trip to the hospital, I had carried Wawerũ a mile from the hospital to the bus stop, and then two more miles from the bus stop to our homestead. And he remained strapped to me even when we rode on the bus, unlike before when I carried him only around our courtyard.

Mother straightened and adjusted his shirtsleeves and collar. Wawerũ looked up at her quizzically, turned toward me, and reached out.

"Have you forgotten me?" she asked. "It's me, your mother."

"He is not sick anymore," I said. "He can walk."

She kept him on the ground. He reached out and tugged on my dress. Determined not to carry him again that day, I took his little hand and put it on Mother's dress. "This is Nyachuru," I said; we all called our mother by her name.

I relaxed, knowing our household would no longer be lonely, as it had been when I left. And Ndurumo and Wanjeri no longer had to cook for us; I preferred Mother's cooking, especially her presence.

As soon as I sat down, my siblings bombarded me with questions. They sat close to me as if they envied me for having gone on such a long safari.

I told them about my bus ride, how makanga handled luggage, and even the musical honks the driver played to alert passengers before the bus arrived at a bus stop. I described jacarandas, Nakuru Town, and its clean people; the nurses and doctors I encountered; the mothers with sick children; and every hospital experience I could remember, including the buttered bread.

But I was nobody's fool. I skipped the entire episode of the cold-water hose and my night accidents. Machira would have had a fun time retelling or needling me about that one. I wanted to wow them, not make them laugh or make fun of our embarrassing behavior.

It was my first time glowing and basking in such limelight. And for the first time, I believed I had matured into a big girl and that my parents could trust me to manage the world around me without them.

44. Mother's Hospital Story

According to my brother Ndurumo, a fact I would learn years later, Waweru and I stayed in the hospital for two weeks, including four days after discharge. But my mother stayed much longer, for almost two months. She returned home three days before my brother and I did.

Two women came to visit her. They returned the following Saturday, accompanied by three others who carried loads of firewood on their backs. Two of the women arrived with water in big metal containers—there were no plastic containers in Solai yet—and food, cooked or uncooked, in chiondo (woven baskets).

This was one of Gĩkũyũ's customs called itega, when women visited a new or recovering mother with food, water, and other supplies. The number of women didn't matter. It could be a large group (after a mother was up and about) or an initial small group of friends to help the new mother regain strength and resume her chores, and to welcome the new baby. A woman or two also helped in a similar way when a woman fell ill.

(This custom has become commercialized and sometimes includes men. Many Kenyans in the diaspora have abandoned itega and adopted Western ways. They celebrate a mother-to-be shower instead of a baby shower.)

Back then, it confused me why the women arranged itega for Mother, even though she had no new baby and was no longer sick.

Whenever women came, Mother made tea while they socialized. Unlike when she had complained that visits wasted too much time, she now took time to tell the women about her sickness that landed her in a sick ward.

When she went to the hospital, one side of her ribcage throbbed and pained her; she could hardly walk. The doctor admitted her so that he could run tests.

After the X-ray, the doctor said liquid had pooled on the inside. He never specified whether it pooled in her lungs or somewhere else.

Before the operation, I overheard a discussion about the problems of operating on her in her condition. I didn't know what that meant. Whatever she suffered from, the doctor decided that not operating on her would put her in more danger.

In the operating room, he made an incision through Mother's ribcage. Using a syringe, he sucked more than half of a small bowl of slimy liquid.

He repeated the same routine a week later.

Besides Mother's sickness, the women traded stories about hospital abuse. Because their stories were hearsay, they wanted to hear Mother's experience, perhaps out of curiosity and, most likely, to confirm their secondhand accounts.

During those exchanges, I learned that although Mother went to the hospital sick, she also gave birth to a baby boy. But she returned home alone.

That intrigued me. What happened to the baby? I wondered.

"Mind the children around," a woman warned Mother when she reached that part.

"What are you doing here?" Mother asked me. "Go join the others outside."

Sometimes I got lucky when Mother called and sent me to get an item. After I took what she wanted, and the women seemed too engrossed in their talk to notice me, I scooted to the side and sat on the floor, my legs drawn up, chin on top, quiet.

I wondered why Mother went to the hospital to "get" a baby, as she did medicine. She got her children at home, with the help of a midwife or two.

During the two births I recalled, I remained confused about where babies came from. First, I believed the midwives brought the baby. Then I wondered how those women got the baby themselves. I agonized about it before I accepted it was unknowable. I needed to wait to learn about it when I became an adult.

But the women's stories about hospital births held my curiosity. I eavesdropped long enough to get a cohesive story.

After about a month and still nursing her ribcage, Mother went into labor. When it intensified, the nurses took her to the labor ward or birthing room with a narrow OBGYN bed, like an examination table—only higher—on which they birthed babies, at least in Nakuru General Hospital. If a potential mother got distracted, she would end up on the cement floor, Mother said. To prevent such an accident, a doctor and a midwife stood on either side of the bed, ready to scoop the new arrival.

In Mother's case, she said, there were two nurses—perhaps a midwife and a nurse. She did not know the difference—medics did not introduce themselves in those days.

During the birthing ordeal, one woman slapped Mother twice on the side of her bare bottom and accused her of failing to push as instructed.

"Call us when you are ready to follow instructions," the midwife said as she and her companion left the room.

"The baby wasn't ready to come," Mother said. "Those sisters became tired of waiting."

In less than half an hour, Mother hollered.

"The baby is coming!"

Her sporadic utterances went unanswered. Her other option was the bell on the wall several feet from the bed that the staff used.

The baby broke through and fell onto the bed. Because of the prolonged labor, it only whimpered, or Mother thought she heard it.

She propped herself on her elbows. But if she reached for the baby, they would both tumble to the floor.

She screamed instead.

On her second scream, the two women burst through the door.

One of them rushed to tend to the baby while the other rang the emergency bell.

The doctor soon arrived.

He put an instrument into the baby's nose and mouth and sucked out fluids. He then held the baby by its ankles and dangled it upside down.

"I watched in disbelief as the doctor mishandled my baby," Mother said, "dangling and slapping his bottom like an object. If I hadn't gone to that hospital, my baby would be alive today."

"Ah!" one woman said. "I'll never step into a hospital to have a baby."

"Never again," Mother said. And she never did.

I wanted to know more. Like, what happened to the baby? Where did he go? But in those days, children never asked questions concerning adult conversations, especially when the adults did not expect them to understand or pay attention. So I carried that story away with me, unfinished, and placed it among the many things I believed I would understand when I grew up.

Years later, as a teenager, I learned that the hospital had taken care of the baby's body.

45. Mami

Our family regrouped, and life resettled, as it always did, and we returned to the business of growing.

As Wawerũ grew older and stronger, he gave my back the break it craved. He cherished his independence and required my attention only when he became tired or hungry. He played with the younger children and trailed the bigger ones, copying whatever they did.

He was not alone.

When my family moved to the village, my siblings and I called our mother by her name, Nyachuru.

For the first year, we never learned that calling our mother by her name went against village culture. This was because we kept to ourselves; children from the village had not yet started coming to our courtyard, except on rare occasions, like when a couple of them came during my first tooth transition.

But when I turned about eight and a half, Mother allowed children from certain families to come to our courtyard to play with us during the day.

I noticed that the children never referred to their mothers by name.

When I said, "Nyachuru doesn't want us to go outside our courtyard."

"Who is that?" They asked in chorus, scowling.

"Nyachuru!" I said, thinking the children did not understand me.

"That's your mother's name?" Several children asked, and one or two paused to give me a side-eye.

"Yes," I said, now puzzled.

Why did they behave as if my mother's name sounded funny or distasteful?

"What kind of name is that?" one child asked and giggled.

Before then, it had never occurred to me that there were un-suitable names. They were just names.

But after I realized the children believed Mother's name was "unacceptable," their reaction after a mere mention of it made me cringe. I quit saying her name in their presence.

Instead of saying, "Nyachuru does not want you coming to our courtyard," I said, "You are not supposed to come to our courtyard."

At the hospital, I noticed that the children who could talk did not call their mothers by name either. Each of them used the title "Mami."

To me, it confirmed that the children in my village knew better than I did.

When Wawerũ and I returned home, the children continued to snicker or give me funny looks when I forgot and mentioned my mother's name. It bothered me so much that something inside me finally gave way.

One evening, Baba and Ndurumo went out to harvest honey. Mother cooked in thingira while my younger siblings and I sat around the fire, waiting for supper and also for the honey. We always got a slice of honeycomb each time Baba brought home honey.

While looking at Mother, without warning, the pressure that must have built and smoldered within me, unbeknownst to me, rose from my chest to my throat, and rushed out, too forceful to hold in or in my mouth.

The word burst out, "Mami!"

Mother paused and glanced at me, then resumed her kitchen work without a word.

Mami—or "Mommy"—was what other children used.

If we were in Gĩkũyũland, I would have called her maitũ, the Gĩkũyũ word for "mother". But somehow, some English terms had seeped in, quietly displacing our own.

The experience felt daunting, my heart racing, like pure labor. I did not attempt another "Mami" that evening. With the pressure released, I wondered how I would manage it afterward.

But from the following day, hesitantly at first, I started calling her Mami. My siblings joined in, one by one, beginning with Gĩthũi and Macharia, the little ones who did not seem to notice the transition.

When Njerũ returned from boarding school, he never mentioned our evolution or respected it. He continued to call Mother "Nyachuru." But one week before his school holiday ended, he switched to "Mami."

My mother became *Mami* for the rest of her life.

To My Readers

Thank you for spending time with my words and for walking with me through these pages that carry the people, places, and moments that shaped my early life. I am deeply grateful you chose to read this book.

If, along the way, you found echoes of your own beginnings, discovered that roots can travel wherever life leads, or recognized the quiet strength it takes to endure change, then this journey has been shared in the truest sense.

—Wanjirũ Warama
Wanjiruwarama.com

Acknowledgements

Many thanks to the members of the West City Writers' Workshop in Point Loma, San Diego, California, for providing a safe forum, offering thoughtful suggestions, and cheering me on.

I am grateful to Timothy Calaway and Margaret McKerrow for reading the manuscript in its early stage and offering suggestions. My deepest thanks go to Mary Thorne Kelley—my cheerleader and proofreader—who has been with me from the beginning of my writing journey. You mean the world to me. Thanks also to Mary Tina Morgan for proofreading the manuscript.

I thank Editor Isabella Furth, whose structural suggestions strengthened and made the book more reader-friendly.

I am indebted to my oldest brother, David Njerũ Warama, for updating me on his hairy childhood escapades, which enriched this book.

I honor my late two brothers: Simon Ndurumo Warama, for clarifying and updating me on our family's history and quirks. This book would not be the same without his input, and John Gĩthũi Warama, who valued my writing so deeply that he used the words *"Your legacy"* before he died. He was a poet in his own right, with several poems published in magazines, though I failed to convince him to write a book about his experience turning a failing high school into a district champion.

My thanks also go to my half-sister, Nancy Wairimũ Warama Mũriũki, for clarifying my father's rocky relationship with his children.

Thanks to my friend Kathy Davis and fellow writer Karl Keating for helping with cover choices, and to Leon Lazarus for his guidance on the mechanics of building a user-friendly website to showcase the book.

Many thanks to Dan Mbuthia, a fellow writer and my cheerleader, who insisted I rebrand this book—a decision that has made it more accessible to readers.

To my Advance Readers: thank you for your time and your honest, independent reviews.

Wanjirũ Warama

About the Author

Wanjirũ Warama was born and raised in Kenya during a time of profound cultural and political change. She later immigrated to California, USA, where she continued her education and built a life shaped by resilience, curiosity, and the power of story.

Her writing preserves the lived experiences of ordinary people whose voices and histories rarely reach the page.

WanjiruWarama.com

Scan Here to Stay Connected: